he **shotokan**
KARATE BIBLE

Acknowledgments

I would like to thank Nita Martin, without whom this book would never have happened. I would also like to thank the following people: Peter Terry and Denzil Fernandes at The Leys School for their help in arranging a venue for the photoshoot; Hiro Omori for supplying the Japanese script; and all those who helped in the photoshoot, Nita Martin, Nick Day, Chris Day, Tom Davidson, Tom Auld, Ben Middleton, Jonathon Burnip and Andrew Kuc.

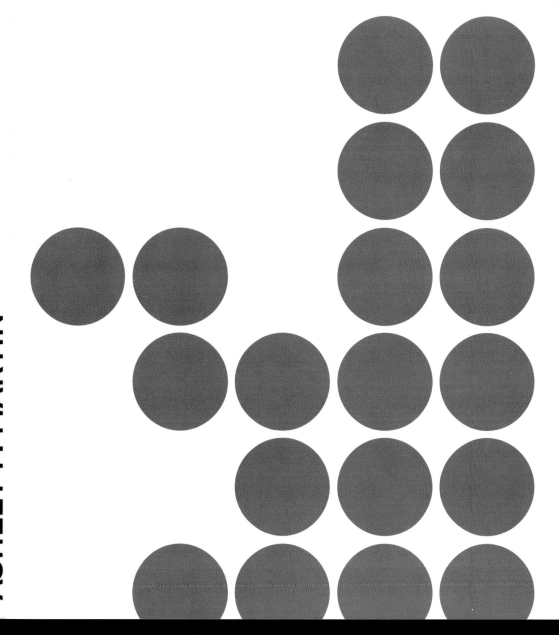

ASHLEY P. MARTIN

the **shotokan**
KARATE BIBLE
BEGINNER TO BLACK BELT

A FIREFLY BOOK

Published by Firefly Books Ltd. 2007

First printing

Publisher Cataloging-in-Publication Data (U.S.)

Martin, Ashley P., 1972–
  The Shotokan karate bible : beginner to black belt /
Ashley P. Martin.
[201] p. : col. photos. ; cm.
Includes bibliographical references and index.
Summary: An authoritative text supporting the newcomer to
karate with all that is needed to know,
up to black belt level.
ISBN-13: 978-1-55407-322-1   (pbk.)
ISBN-10: 1-55407-322-7   (pbk.)
    1. Karate. I. Title.
796.815/3 dc22   GV1114.3.M378   2007

Library and Archives Canada Cataloguing in Publication

Martin, Ashley P., 1972–
  The Shotokan karate Bible : beginner to black belt /
Ashley P. Martin.
Includes bibliographical references and index.
ISBN-13: 978-1-55407-322-1
ISBN-10: 1-55407-322-7
    1. Karate. I. Title.
GV1114.3.M375 2007   796.815'3   C2007-902493-9

Note: It is always the responsibility of the individual to assess his or her own fitness capability before participating in any training activity. Whilst every effort has been made to ensure the content of this book is as technically accurate as possible, neither the author nor the publishers can accept responsibility for any injury or loss sustained as a result of the use of this material.

Published in the United States by
Firefly Books (U.S.) Inc.
P.O. Box 1338, Ellicott Station
Buffalo, New York 14205

Published in Canada by
Firefly Books Ltd.
66 Leek Crescent
Richmond Hill, Ontario L4B 1H1

Text and cover design by James Watson
Printed in Singapore

Contents

CHAPTER **ONE** introduction

Karate is a Japanese martial art based on techniques developed in Okinawa and China that focuses on self-defense using punches, kicks and blocks. Despite this emphasis, other techniques, such as joint locks, throws and leg sweeps, are also included in the system. Karate is one of the few martial arts to contain such a wide range of techniques.

This book is aimed at the student of shotokan karate. There are many styles of karate, for example, goju-ryu, wado-ryu and shito-ryu, but ultimately each style of karate teaches the same principles, just with a different emphasis. A punch is still a punch, a kick is still a kick.

The Shotokan Karate Bible is intended to be a guide for the karate student, from beginner right through to expert, when you would be tested to receive the coveted black belt. Studying from a book is no substitute for a good teacher, but it can complement training with a qualified instructor.

What Does Karate Mean?

Karate, written in kanji

Written in kanji, Japanese pictographs, the word karate is composed of two characters. The first, pronounced kara, means 'empty' and has Zen connotations. The second pictograph, pronounced te, means 'hand,' so karate can be translated as 'empty hand.'

The kara symbol is thought to have its origins in the Buddhist sunyata, the Sanskrit term for the ancient metaphysical concept of emptiness or nothingness. Gichin Funakoshi, the father of modern karate, wrote:

> As a mirror's polished surface reflects whatever stands before it and a quiet valley carries even small sounds, so must the student of Karate-Do render their mind empty of selfishness and wickedness in an effort to react appropriately toward anything they might encounter. This is the meaning of the kara or "empty" of Karate-Do.

Funakoshi is saying that you need to empty your mind in order to take the most appropriate action. He is implying that the appropriate action is the righteous and moral thing to do. However, many take it to mean the correct action to take in order to succeed in a fight. If you clutter your mind, you can't think clearly. Thus, an empty mind is needed to practice good karate.

This, however, is not the original meaning of karate. The original pictograph for kara was quite different. In Japanese, it was a homonym: that's to say, it was pronounced in the same way, but it had a different meaning. It meant Tang, which was a Chinese imperial dynasty at the zenith of Chinese civilization that had a huge cultural influence on its neighbors. Tang was synonymous with China, and the original karate pictographs meant 'Chinese

Original form of karate, written in kanji

hand.' In Okinawa, the same two pictographs were pronounced tode, and many in Okinawa referred to them simply as te, meaning hand.

This change from the old ideographs for karate to the new occurred at the beginning of the 20th century. Japan was very nationalistic at this time, and for many, the association of the old symbol with China was not acceptable. Some karate schools, particularly in Tokyo, began writing karate with hiragana, Japanese phonetic characters, as a way of avoiding the 'inappropriate' kanji with its Chinese connotation. Others had started writing 'empty hand' using the new symbol for kara. At a meeting of Okinawan karate masters in 1936, the new way of writing karate was officially accepted.

History of Karate

Much of the history of karate is shrouded in mystery. This is sometimes explained as being a consequence of the fact that, before the 20th century, martial arts were often practiced in secret societies. But a more significant factor seems to be the impact of the 'Typhoon of Steel,' the invasion of Okinawa in 1945 by American forces that completely flattened the cities of Naha and Shuri, destroying any written records of karate's early development.

An examination of the available details suggests a fascinating origin for karate in Okinawa: a crack team of royal bodyguards, a kind of 19th-century secret service, working as bureaucrats and palace officials by day and developing and practicing a deadly unarmed fighting style by night.

CHINESE WAY OF THE FIST

Many accounts of the origin of karate trace its roots back to ancient China with the introduction of martial exercises into the Shaolin temple by a Buddhist monk called Bodhidharma in the sixth century. He traveled from India to the Shaolin temple in China and found the resident monks to be in a feeble condition. Bodhidharma instructed the monks in the courtyard and began to teach them the art of Shih Pa Lohan Sho (the 18 hands of Lohan) so that the monks could attain spiritual enlightenment while preserving their physical health.

This story may be more myth than history, but the Shaolin temple was certainly one source of the class of Chinese martial arts known as ch'uan fa, the way of the fist. Chinese ch'uan fa was certainly a major influence on the martial art that we today call karate. But few of the Chinese traditions have been continued by karate practitioners. To find the real birth place of karate, we need to look at a small island in the East China Sea called Okinawa.

KARATE: AN OKINAWAN MARTIAL ART

Okinawa is the largest of the Ryukyu Islands, an island chain that extends 1,000 km from southern Japan to

The Ryukyu Islands are located in the East China Sea

Taiwan. Today, Okinawa Island is the capital of the Japanese Okinawa Prefecture, but it was once an independent nation with a separate language and culture.

Martial arts probably existed in Okinawa as early as the Chinese Tang Dynasty (618–906 AD), but they would have been quite different from the karate that we see today. Okinawa entered into a tributary relationship with China in 1372, which meant that Okinawa was a province of China and would send regular taxes to the Chinese emperor. This relationship accelerated Chinese influences on Okinawan culture. There was a permanent Chinese mission resident in the Okinawan Royal Palace, and many of the officials brought with them ch'uan fa secrets. At this stage, it would have been a distinctly Chinese martial art.

A common misconception is that karate was started in Okinawa by peasants. Learning a martial art like karate takes a great deal of time and effort. Peasants spent all their time during the day working, often doing back-breaking work. It would take an extraordinary person to then engage in something as physically demanding as karate in the evening. In fact, the karate masters were invariably of the keimochi (noble) class.

Three cities on Okinawa are important to the story of karate's development: Naha, a large port; Tomari, a smaller port; and the royal city of Shuri, the capital city of Okinawa. Each city had karate masters with their own kata and traditions.

The karate that developed at Naha, known as Naha-te, can be characterized as being a soft-style martial art, using more circular hand and foot movements that flow from one to another, giving it a graceful appearance.

Karate that follows the Shuri-te tradition is described as a hard-style martial art and tends to use big, strong, linear movements. In the 1500s, the King Sho Shen had a castle built in Shuri, to act as his palace and the bureaucratic center of his kingdom. It was here that the linear karate, which would become shotokan karate, developed.

THE STYLES OF KARATE		
Style of Karate	*Founder*	*In the tradition of*
Shotokan	Gichin Funakoshi	Shuri-te
Goju-ryu	Chogun Miyagi	Naha-te
Shito-ryu	Kenwa Mabuni	Shuri-te and Naha-te

The Tomari traditions were rather similar to the Shuri traditions, largely due to the fact that many of the Tomari masters were originally from Shuri, having retired from royal service.

Naha-te and Shuri-te have quite different histories and origins. Our interest is in the development of shotokan karate, so our attention will focus on the events that unfolded in Shuri.

Two key events occurred that made Okinawa a unique breeding ground for a new martial art:

- In 1429, Okinawa was unified under the first Sho Dynasty. Prior to this, Okinawa had suffered from internal conflict between warring clans. To help maintain order, the second Sho King, Sho Shin, disarmed the bickering warlords by introducing a weapons ban. The nobility, the keimochi, were instead set to work as bureaucrats.

- In 1609, the Japanese Satsuma Clan of Kyushu invaded Okinawa. They probably found the weapons ban quite convenient and ordered that it be continued. Only now the ban was enforced by the Satsuma Samura, who wielded katana, the deadly Japanese longsword.

By 1650, the Japanese were operating a policy of National Seclusion, Sakoku, which barred Westerners from trading in Japan (with an exception for limited trade with the Dutch). This policy was extended to Okinawa. Officially, Okinawa was still a province of China, so to keep control of Okinawa while avoiding war with China, the Shuri officials were ordered to deny any connection with Japan.

To compound this situation, European and American ships started appearing on the Okinawan shores in the

19th century in the form of explorers, missionaries and whalers. This conflicted with the Japanese isolationism and put the officials at Shuri in a difficult and dangerous position. They were instructed not to allow trade with the Westerners but were also not permitted to explain that the king of Okinawa was subordinate to the Japanese.

Matters came to a head in 1853 when Commodore Matthew Perry of the United States Navy paid a visit to Okinawa. His objective was to open trade between Japan and the United States. He decided that a show of strength in Okinawa was needed as a prelude to his negotiations in Japan itself. Perry demanded that he be allowed to see the king to discuss a trade agreement. As usual, the Okinawan officials politely declined. Perry then landed a force of 200 marines armed with Springfield rifle-muskets, two cannons and two brass bands and paraded up to Shuri castle. Perry himself traveled on a sedan chair carried by Chinese coolies.

Perry and his entourage marched up to the gates of the royal palace and demanded entry. The Shuri officials allowed him to enter the main hall, where he found the regent and a small group of his staff. The Okinawans expected Perry to declare himself governor of Okinawa, but Perry had only planned to demonstrate his strength, and having made his point, he returned to his ship. It was a tense incident nonetheless, and coming face to face with 200 marines must have had an impact on the staff at Shuri. And as so many of the karate masters of that day were employed as high-ranking members of the royal household, it is very likely that they would have been there facing Perry and his men.

Clayton (2004) suggests that this encounter at Shuri Castle, combined perhaps with the many presumed incidents that remain undocumented, had a fundamental influence on the development of karate. He suggests that karate was designed to deal with a 'target rich' environment, which is to say that it is meant to be effective even when outnumbered and surrounded by opponents. He concluded the following:

- Spending more than a few seconds fighting each opponent would not be good enough; they would have to be dispatched very rapidly.
- Ground fighting would be suicide.
- Defending against opponents armed with firearms or swords was necessary.

SATUNISHI 'TODE' SAKUGAWA (1733–1815)

Sakugawa studied under an Okinawan master of tode called Takahara. He learned White Crane style ch'uan fa from Kong Su Kung, the Chinese military attache to the Okinawan court. (The name of this Chinese dignitary is a matter of controversy: Kong Su Kung might not have been his name but instead his rank.)

The Okinawan reading of the ideographs of Kong Su Kung can be read Kushanku, and Sakugawa is often credited with having created the kata Kushanku, which would later form the basis of the shotokan kata Kanku Dai and Kanku Sho. In shotokan karate, Kanku Dai is the 'master' kata. It appears to contain segments from all the core shotokan kata and may well have been the precursor of the Heian kata.

Sakugawa is sometimes credited with creating the dojo kun, the school code, but more commonly it is attributed instead to Gichin Funakoshi. The dojo kun is recited in many karate schools to this day. Its most literal translation reads:

Each seek perfection of character
Each protect the way of truth
Each foster the spirit of effort
Each respect others
Each guard against impetuous courage

Perhaps Sakugawa's greatest legacy was his most famous student, Sokon Matsumura.

SOKON 'BUSHI' MATSUMURA (1797–1893)
The Bodyguard

If there was one man responsible for the transformation of Okinawa-te from what was essentially a Chinese art to the new art of karate, it was Sokon Matsumura.

Matsumura started training with Sakugawa at the age of 14. He was determined to become the greatest fighter in the land. He went on to become master of military affairs in the royal court, a highly important position as it would have meant that he was responsible for the safety of the king. After the capture of Okinawa by the Satsuma Clan, the king was required to spend half the year in Kyushu. Naturally, Matsumura traveled with the king, and it was during this time that Matsumura learned the sword-fighting art of Jigen Ryu Kenjutsu.

Legend has it that Matsumura was given the title Bushi, meaning warrior, by King Sho Ko after he fought a bull unarmed. The king had announced that, as entertainment, his great bodyguard, Matsumura, would battle a raging bull (some accounts say that the bull was a present from the emperor of Japan). Everyone was invited to watch the great spectacle. Matsumura had to accept the challenge or lose face. On the appointed day, he turned up to face the bull. He stared into the bull's eyes, and it turned around and bolted. He had defeated the bull just by looking at it!

Matsumura had accomplished this apparent miracle by careful preparation. On discovering the impossible task he had been set, he went to visit the bull, taking with him a long pin. He looked into the eyes of the bull and poked it on the nose. He repeated this every day, up to the day of the challenge. He thus trained the bull to fear his gaze and so actually won through careful planning.

Over time Matsumura served as chief bodyguard to a total of three Okinawan kings: King Sho Ko, King Sho Iku and King Sho Tai. All three of these kings were deposed by their Japanese masters. The last, Sho Tai, was ousted at the beginning of the Meiji Restoration when the Kingdom of Ryukyu became the Okinawa Prefecture. Sho Tai was abducted and taken to Japan, where he lived out his final days in exile. The aristocracy was abolished, and this would have put Matsumura and all the other Shuri officials out of work.

Matsumura would have been in service at the time that Perry made his historic visit to Shuri, and given his position, it is quite likely that he would have been in that hall standing at the regent's side facing 200 marines. This event may have influenced the direction of Matsumura's training and so have helped shape modern karate.

ANKO ITOSU (1830–1915)
The Big Kata Man

Itosu worked alongside Matsumura as secretary and translator to the king of Okinawa. But he was also, presumably, an apprentice bodyguard to the king under Matsumura. He trained and worked alongside Matsumura for 30 years.

Itosu was heavily built and had a reputation both for being very strong and for being able to withstand heavy blows. Funakoshi says that he had 'the silhouette of a barrel' and that he could crush bamboo with his bare hands.

In 1901 Itosu introduced karate into the physical education system at an elementary school in Shuri. This was the same year that King Sho Tai died in exile, and it is possible that this was no coincidence. Once there was no chance that the king would return, perhaps Itosu felt released from any vows of secrecy he had taken while a royal bodyguard.

In 1908 he wrote a letter to the Prefecture Educational Department outlining the benefits that karate had to offer and encouraging the introduction of karate into all Okinawan schools. His suggestion was well-received, and karate became part of the school curriculum in Okinawa. This made karate instruction available to the masses for the first time: the veil of secrecy over karate had been well and truly lifted.

Itosu's greatest legacy is his contribution to karate kata. He decided that some relatively easy kata were needed for teaching to middle school students. He invented the Pinan kata, which in the shotokan system are known as the Heian kata. These kata were possibly based on the Kanku kata, combined with moves from a long-forgotten kata called Chanan. Other kata that Itosu is reputed to have created are Naifanchi Nidan and Sandan, which later became known as Tekki Nidan and Sandan. An alternative theory is that the three Tekki kata were originally one long kata and that Itosu split them up. He also standardized the versions of Kanku Sho and Kanku Dai that are based on the kata Kushanku.

ANKO AZATO (1828–1906)
The Invisible Man of Karate

It seems that there are no surviving pictures of Azato and very little is written about him, which makes him a bit of a mystery man. Most of what we know comes from the writings of Gichin Funakoshi, who referred to Azato as the best martial artist he had ever met.

Like Itosu, Azato was one of Matsumura's students and held the position of foreign affairs advisor within the Shuri Royal Court. He was a member of the aristocracy. He owned a castle and was a hereditary lord of the Azato village.

Funakoshi tells us that Azato challenged an armed sword master to a duel and defeated him with his bare hands by deflecting the sword with his arm before immobilizing his opponent. In another story, Azato and Itosu were confronted by 30 men, so they fled into a nearby house. The men swarmed around the house, and the two decided that a fight was unavoidable. Azato leaped out the window and started dispatching one hoodlum after another using a single blow each time, while Itosu dealt with the men around the other side of the house.

What is notable about this story is that it mentions that Azato and Itosu were using what is today called ikken hissatsu, one deadly strike, which represents the ability to defeat an opponent with a single devastating attack. This is one of the defining characteristics of modern shotokan karate.

Karate: A Japanese Martial Art

GICHIN 'SHOTO' FUNAKOSHI (1868–1957)
The Father of Japanese Karate

Gichin Funakoshi was the school teacher from Shuri who is credited with bringing karate to Japan, thus earning himself the title of 'Father of Modern Karate' (or sometimes 'Father of Japanese Karate'). In fact, he wasn't alone in bringing karate to Japan. Many karate masters from Okinawa traveled to Japan to promote their art, including Kenwa Mabuni, founder of shito-ryu, which is a synthesis of Shuri-te and Naha-te, and Chojun Miyagi, founder of goju-ryu, which is based on the Naha-te traditions. But it was Funakoshi who did it first and perhaps did the better job of promoting it.

Funakoshi started studying karate under Anko Azato and later studied under Itosu. Funakoshi recalls that he spent 10 years learning the three Naihanchi (Tekki) kata under Itosu. In 1913, as chairman of the Shobukai, the martial arts association of Okinawa, Funakoshi organized a group to travel around Okinawa performing public demonstrations of karate. It wasn't until 1916 that he was able to take karate to Japan, where he demonstrated at the Butokuden, the official center of Japanese martial arts. This event, and the demonstrations that followed, helped to bolster the popularity of the art. However, it was the visit of the crown prince of Japan, Hirohito, that really raised the profile of karate, and in 1922 Funakoshi was invited by the Japanese Education Ministry to demonstrate karate at the first All Japan Athletic Exhibition in Tokyo. During his time in Japan, he stayed as a guest of Jigoro Kano, the creator of judo, and taught at the Kodokan, the judo school.

At the time that Funakoshi brought karate to Japan, the country was going through a very nationalistic phase, and anything that was not considered to be pure Japanese was regarded with suspicion or contempt. Karate of course was of Chinese and Okinawan origin. To overcome this perception, Funakoshi portrayed karate as following the Japanese budo (martial) tradition and made the following changes:

- The first ideograph in kara-te was changed from the old one that represented China to a new one meaning empty.

- Funakoshi adopted the uniforms and belt system of Kano's judo. Before this, there was no such thing as a karate black belt.

- Chinese culture was viewed with suspicion, but Zen Buddhism was not. Zen had a great deal of influence on Japanese culture and was considered an important part of Japanese budo. Karate's Shaolin origins were therefore emphasized alongside the adoption of the Zen-like kara ideograph associating it with Zen Buddhism. This link was somewhat spurious because karate's development had been tied for so long to Okinawa, which had never really adopted Buddhism in the same way as Japan.

- Funakoshi attempted to change the kata names to Japanese words. For example, he renamed the Naihanchi kata to Tekki, but only a few of these new names persisted into the next generation of karate instructors, Funakoshi's own son included. Perhaps for them, the exotic Chinese or Okinawan names just had more flavor than the (from their point of view) mundane Japanese-sounding names.

Funakoshi invented the Taikyoku Kata and Ten No Kata, which were even simpler versions of Itosu's Pinan (Heian) kata, for teaching to elementary school students. However, according to one of Funakoshi's students, Shigeru Egami, these kata were in fact created by Funakoshi's son, Yoshitaka.

By 1935 Funakoshi had sufficient financial backing to build the first karate dojo, or training hall, in Japan. It became known as the Shotokan, after Funakoshi's pen name, shoto literally meaning 'pine waves' and kan meaning 'house.'

SHOTOKAN KATA NAMES		
Okinawan/Chinese Name	Funakoshi's New Japanese Name	Modern Shotokan Name
Pinan	Heian	Heian
Naihanchi	Tekki	Tekki
Seisan	Hangetsu	Hangetsu
Chinto	Gankaku	Gankaku
Niseishi	Nijushiho	Nijushiho
Wanshu	Empi	Empi
Rohai	Meikyo	Meikyo
Useishi	Hotaku	Gojushiho
Ji'in	Shokyo	Ji'in
Sochin	Hakko	Sochin
Chinte	Shoin	Chinte

YOSHITAKA 'GIGO' FUNAKOSHI (1906–1945)

The Young Teacher

Gichin Funakoshi started the transformation of karate from an Okinawan to a Japanese art, but these changes were primarily ones of philosophy and nomenclature. However, Funakoshi's son, Yoshitaka (or Gigo, using a different reading of the ideographs for his name), really did transform the techniques of karate to produce what is essentially the shotokan karate that we practice today.

At a very young age, Yoshitaka was diagnosed as having tuberculosis, a terrible disease that, in 1913, was effectively a death sentence. Despite this, he engaged in his karate practice with great energy and spirit. He used very low, long stances and had a great love of sparring. He is said to have been responsible for the introduction of the side kicks, yoko kekomi and yoko keage, and the roundhouse kick, mawashi-geri, into the shotokan karate system.

The two Funakoshis shared the teaching at the Shotokan. The softly spoken Gichin would teach his karate with high stances in the afternoon. The spirited and outspoken Yoshitaka, who was referred to by the students as waka sensei, young teacher, would teach his low stances, big punches and high kicks in the evening. Yoshitaka sadly succumbed to a lung infection in 1945 and died. Despite this, it is clear that it is Yoshitaka's method that lives on in modern shotokan karate.

THE KARATE CORPORATION

Following the Second World War, the occupying American forces placed a ban on martial arts in Japan because they were thought to have fostered regimentation and militarism. Karate managed to continue largely due to its emphasis on being a do, a way of life, which had spiritual goals and positive health applications rather than militaristic objectives.

There was a great deal of interest in karate from Allied servicemen stationed in Japan, and many of them trained with karate schools there and then took this strange new art back to their home countries. In 1953, the US Air Force invited Hidetaka Nishiyama on a sponsored tour of air bases in mainland United States to teach special courses for the personnel.

The other contributing factor in karate's rapid postwar expansion into the rest of the world was the emigration of karate masters from Japan and Okinawa. One organization that was active in this expansion was the Nihon Karate Kyokai, the Japan Karate Association (JKA), which was founded in 1948 with Funakoshi named as chief instructor. At that time, the JKA was based on the clubs studying Funakoshi's karate in the Tokyo area, and in fact almost all the senior JKA members were from the university clubs of Takushoku, Waseda and Keio. Karate quickly spread under the JKA as it actively promoted karate worldwide by sending the graduates of its instructor training program all over the world.

SHOTOKAN SPLITS

In 1957 Gichin Funakoshi passed away. He did not name a successor, and his students split into two groups. One group called themselves shotokai (meaning Shoto's Group) and were led by Shigeru Egami. They were traditionalists who did not approve of the commercialization of karate or the growing popularity of competitive karate. The other group was the more radical JKA, led by Masatoshi Nakayama, who referred to their style as shotokan. The JKA promoted competition and organized the first Japanese karate championship in 1957.

It was in 1986 that the then head of the JKA, Masatoshi Nakayama, passed away and leadership was passed to Nobuyuki Nakahara. However, his appointment was challenged by a number of JKA masters. Subsequent political infighting led to a major split resulting in two main factions: one led by Tetsuhiko Asai, who appointed Mikio Yahara as chief instructor, and the other headed by Nakahara, who named Motokuni Sugiura chief instructor.

Following the split, legal disputes continued for many years over everything including who could legally use the JKA name and who had ownership of the headquarters building, the JKA Honbu. So for a period there was a peculiar situation in which two groups called themselves the JKA. In 1999 the Sugiura group won the exclusive right to the JKA name in Japan, and the Asai group renamed themselves Japan Karate Shotokai (JKS).

The political infighting is largely irrelevant to the many people practicing karate throughout the world. There are too many karate associations to count, but they do broadly practice the same karate techniques and follow the same customs that were taught by Funakoshi and son in Tokyo at the beginning of the 20th century.

CHAPTER **TWO** beginner's guide

The typical karate class involves rows of white uniformed students moving up and down a hall punching, kicking and shouting, with an instructor giving instructions in Japanese. This chapter explains many of the customs traditionally followed in karate classes and some of the terms used when talking about karate.

The Uniform

The karate uniform, which is called a dogi or more commonly just a gi, is traditionally made of white cotton. The karate gi is based on the judo gi but over the years has evolved from the heavyweight material of the judo gi into a lighter uniform. The karate gi also has ties on both sides of the jacket, which are not present on the judo gi. When tied up, they help to keep the uniform together. The judo gi is held together solely by the belt.

Because of the karate uniform's lighter weight, it cannot take the same punishment as the judo gi. If someone grabs your jacket and tries to throw you, the karate gi may tear. One way to avoid this is to leave the ties untied, which will tend to result in the jacket just getting pulled out of the belt but not tearing.

Many karate schools will insist that students wear an ironed gi. The key is to look tidy!

The Karate Tripos: Kihon, Kata and Kumite

Karate practice can be considered to consist of three components: kihon, kata and kumite.

Kihon means 'basic.' When you practice kihon, you

The karate uniform is called a dogi

focus on repeating the basic techniques that form the foundation of all the other elements of karate. Often kihon involves moving up and down the training hall performing a single technique or a short combination of techniques.

Kata means 'form' or 'pattern.' In the context of karate, this means a sequence of prearranged techniques against imaginary opponents. Traditional karate styles are largely defined by their kata. There are two approaches to viewing kata. One is to view it as a performance art where the kata is performed purely for its own sake and where the aesthetics of the form are paramount. The other approach is to view the kata as a catalogue of fighting moves that have some practical application for self-defense.

Kumite means 'sparring' and is performed with a training partner. At the beginner level, this consists of basic five-step sparring (kihon gohon kumite) and basic one-step sparring (kihon ippon kumite). These are performed using formal positions and prearranged attacks and defenses. At the advanced level, this develops into free one-attack sparring (jiyu ippon kumite), where the positions are less formal, but the attacks are still prearranged.

The most advanced level of kumite practice is free sparring, jiyu kumite, in which anything goes as long as it's within the realms of safety. This is also sometimes referred to as randori, which translates as 'disordered engagement.' A common and safe form of free sparring is practiced at slow speed but is continuous, and all techniques are allowed, including grabs, elbow strikes and throws. A more common form of free sparring, sometimes called shiai kumite, tournament sparring, is done with full-speed techniques but with restrictive rules on what techniques can be used and with interruptions each time a point is scored.

Dojo Etiquette

Karate begins with a bow and ends with a bow
The karate training hall is called the dojo, which literally translated means 'place of the way.' Some karate schools use a dojo that is for the sole purpose of karate training, but most dojos are sports halls that are only used part time by a karate school. Whatever its physical nature, within the karate dojo you will be expected to follow certain rules of conduct.

GENERAL BEHAVIOR

Practicing karate should be fun, but it should none-theless be remembered that some of the activities can be dangerous if done casually and with complacency. Therefore, always treat your teacher and your fellow students with respect:

- Keep toe and finger nails short.

- Do not wear jewellery during training.

- Keep your training uniform clean and in good condition.

- Show respect to each other by not talking, swearing or disrupting the lesson.

PARTNER WORK

- When training with a partner, the objective is mutual improvement of your karate, not to hurt each other.

- Never lose your temper.

- Always show control. You should never cause injury to your partner.

THE INSTRUCTOR

- Show your instructor respect. As a sign of respect, you should refer to your instructor as sensei, which means teacher.

- Pay attention to what your instructor tells you and be especially mindful of instructions regarding safety.

- If you are late for a session, wait for the instructor to indicate that you may join in.

BOWING

Bowing is very common in karate classes. In some schools, there is a bow every few minutes. In other schools, there are almost no bows. The most important times to bow are as follows:

- At the beginning and end of the class.

- At the beginning and end of a kata performance.

- Before you start sparring with a partner and then at the end when you are finished sparring.

- Whenever your instructor tells you to bow. This might be with the instruction rei, which means bow.

1

2

3

Several types of bow are used in Japanese culture. The most common bow in the karate class is the standing bow.

1   Start with your heels together. This is musubi-dachi (literally meaning 'connected stance').

2   Keeping your hands at your sides and your back straight, gently bend from the waist.

3   Complete the bow by straightening up again.

Partly due to the influence of Bruce Lee in the film *Enter the Dragon*, there is a belief that you should keep your eyes on your partner while you bow. If you do not trust someone enough to take your eyes off them, you should not be bowing to them at all!

Training Tips

To make good progress, the karate student should train in the dojo with an experienced instructor at least two hours per week. For the beginner, three or four hours per week is optimal. Generally, more than eight hours per week of intense training can be counterproductive because it may result in injuries.

Before engaging in intense training, always warm up as detailed below.

STRETCHING

Stretching defines your freedom of movement. Lack of suitable flexibility can mean working against your own muscles as they reach the limits of their normal range. Good flexibility is essential for correct stances and effective kicks and to minimize muscle strains and injuries. For best results, try to stretch for 20–30 minutes per day.

STRENGTHENING

Strong legs are especially important in karate because they are the driving force behind all techniques. High kicks require not only flexibility but also strong legs and stomach muscles.

FITNESS

Improve your cardiovascular fitness through aerobic activities like jogging or cycling.

KEEP A TRAINING DIARY

Use a training diary to keep a record of what you have learned. Keeping a note of important points will help you to remember them. Often the significance may not be obvious until later. When you do have a question about how best to do a technique, you can look back through your journal to see if you previously had the answer. You should also keep a note of any unanswered questions. Later you can look for an opportunity to find an answer. Often an instructor will ask, 'Any questions?' Rarely does anyone have a question, but they should! If you have your questions ready in advance, you can take this opportunity to learn.

Kiai: The Martial Shout

Karate classes contain a lot of shouting. The martial shout used in karate is called a kiai, which literally translated means 'spirit unity.' It is comparable with the 'grunt' used by tennis players when hitting the ball. Monica Seles was renowned for her grunt. Many players complained about it putting them off or disguising the sound of her racket hitting the ball, but she felt that the grunting simply helped her to generate more power in her shots. In karate, the kiai is indeed also used to distract the opponent as well as to help focus power. You should use kiai for the following reasons:

■ To boost your confidence by psyching yourself up before a fight.

■ To intimidate or unsettle an opponent.

■ To help with breathing. Holding your breath while attacking is a common mistake, and shouting a kiai on the technique ensures a smooth exhalation.

The karate kiai is a martial shout

When uttering a kiai, you shouldn't be saying a specific word. Don't yell out 'Kiai!' This would be a bit like screaming 'Shout!' Ideally, avoid consonants altogether: something like 'Ai!' or 'Eia!' is best.

There are a number of circumstances when it is appropriate to use a kiai, and some where it is positively required:

- Shotokan kata typically contain two kiai points. The kiai is considered a technique in itself, and omitting it is a mistake.

- Use kiai at the beginning of a fight to boost your confidence and intimidate your opponent.

- Use kiai during sparring when you score a technique.

- During gradings, it is important to show strong spirit. Use kiai on the last technique of a sequence.

- Use kiai whenever your instructor tells you to.

Kime: The Art of Focus

Kime literally means 'decision.' In karate, it means to focus all one's strength and energy into each technique. *Kime-waza* means a decisive technique, one that would finish a fight in a single blow. Good karate consists of only decisive techniques, and this includes not just punches and kicks but also blocks. Thus, all karate techniques are explosive and are delivered with maximum intensity in the shortest time possible. The only exception to this is when a technique is meant to be delivered at slow speed. In this case, the moves should be performed under tension in a slow, controlled manner. But these moves are not without kime: the kime is merely spread throughout the technique.

Distancing

Upon completion of a karate technique, the body's motion is abruptly halted and the final position held. This is accomplished by instantaneously tensing all the muscles of the body, coupled with exhaling at the point of completion of the technique. The tension is only momentary, and you should immediately relax the muscles. It is important that this tension only happens at the end of the technique: tensing the muscles when they are not needed will only slow down techniques.

This tensing of the body is often incorrectly called kime, but in fact the kime occurs before this. The point of kime, of decision, is the point where you make contact with your target, not at the point of maximum extension. Misunderstanding this results in techniques that might look and even feel strong but are actually ineffective. The correct distancing for decisive techniques should be practiced by using a punching bag. When aiming techniques at your training partner, you should not use this distancing precisely because you do not want to injure them. In this situation, you should focus the technique so that it comes to a halt just before it makes contact.

1 Too near to the target. The arm has not had enough time to acquire its full speed, resulting in a weaker punch.

2 Too far from the target. The arm has reached the end of its extension and has been slowed down by itself. This *is* the distancing you should use when training with a partner.

3 Correct distancing. Contact should be made with the arm at about 70 percent extension.

1   2   3

Kata Performance

SPEED

In the basic kata, all individual techniques are intended to be fast moves. Each technique should be performed with explosive speed, starting and stopping abruptly. In between each move, relax and prepare mentally and physically for the next explosive move.

MOVES SHOULD BECOME NATURAL

The advanced practitioner can perform kata almost without thinking. Through the constant repetition of kata, reactions are built up over time so that when a particular technique is needed, it is instinctive. The moves in the kata encode techniques with practical self-defense applications. In real situations, there will not be enough time to think, only time to react. You should therefore practice kata every day. This may simply involve running through the kata in your mind as this will still help make the kata instinctive.

CORRECT FORM

Maintain the correct positioning of the stance and hand techniques. You must learn to be observant of small details and be able to reproduce what your teacher does.

MENTAL FOCUS

When you practice your kata, you should picture imaginary opponents. This will help you think about the meaning of the moves. Appear alert and perform with strong spirit: each move should be executed with conviction and passion. Look in the direction that you attack, and when you kiai, do it with spirit.

Japanese Commands

In karate classes, it is common to give some instructions in Japanese, even though it may not be the first language of the instructor or the students. This will vary from one karate school to another. Some instructors do not use any Japanese, but most will use at least some. The table on page 16 is a guide to some common instructions given in Japanese.

In addition to these, the instructor may also use Japanese terms for the various techniques used in karate. These terms are introduced throughout this book, and a summary can be found in the glossary.

Meditation

Some karate schools, generally the more traditional ones, have a period of meditation at the beginning and the end of the class. Some will only have meditation at the beginning or only at the end. Many schools will omit meditation altogether. The format of this meditation period varies, but typically it is as follows:

1 The class lines up.

2 The instructor (or often the senior grade) says 'Seiza.' Seiza literally translated means correct sitting and is a kneeling position with the feet tucked under the buttocks.

3 The instructor announces 'Mokuso,' which means to meditate. At this point, you should place your left hand in your right with the palms up. In many karate schools, you should close your eyes, while other

COMMON JAPANESE KARATE TERMS		
Japanese	*Meaning*	*Comments*
Hajime	Begin	Used in tournaments to start the fight or in class to start a combination.
Rei	Bow	
Seiretsu	Line up	In most classes you will be expected to line up in grade order.
Naore	Relax (literally translated as 'put back into place')	Return to ready stance and remain ready for the next instruction.
Otaigai ni	Face each other	
Sensei ni	Face the teacher	
Shomen ni	Face the front	
Mawatte	Turn around	Used in line work when the class runs out of space and it is time to go back the other way.
Yoi	Ready	Stand in ready stance and await the next instruction.
Yame	Stop	
Yasume	Rest	

schools expect you to lower your eyes, focusing on the ground just in front of you.

4 You should meditate by relaxing and clearing your mind. This continues, typically for between 10 and 60 seconds, until the instructor announces 'Mokuso yame,' which means 'meditation finished.'

Meditation is performed in the seiza position

The meditation period at the beginning of the lesson is useful to put you in the correct mind-set to begin training, allowing you to clear your mind of needless clutter. The meditation should leave you calm, relaxed and focused. The meditation at the end of a lesson allows you to reflect on what you have learned.

The Belt System

The color of the karate belt signifies the grade of the wearer. The belt colors for each grade vary from organization to organization, but they always start at white and end at black. The following system is used in this book:

SHOTOKAN BELT SYSTEM

Grade	Japanese	Belt Color
Ungraded		White
9th Kyu	kukyu	Orange
8th Kyu	hachikyu	Red
7th Kyu	shichikyu	Yellow
6th Kyu	rokyu	Green
5th Kyu	gokyu	Purple
4th Kyu	yonkyu	Purple with one white stripe
3rd Kyu	sankyu	Brown
2nd Kyu	nikyu	Brown with one white stripe
1st Kyu	ikkyu	Brown with two white stripes
1st Dan	shodan	Black
2nd Dan	nidan	Black
3rd Dan	sandan	Black
4th Dan	yondan	Black
5th Dan	godan	Black
6th Dan	rokudan	Black
7th Dan	sichidan	Black
8th Dan	hachidan	Black
9th Dan	kudan	Black
10th Dan	judan	Black

The color of the karate belt signifies grade

An enduring myth about the belt colors is that they originate from the belt changing color with age. The story tells us that the founders of karate never washed their belts. All their belts started out white, but as they were used, they grew discolored with sweat, grass stains and dirt, first becoming yellow and then going from green to brown and then finally to black.

It is a seductive story but certainly untrue. Apart from the fact that the belts would have been disgusting and smelly, it just wouldn't work – the belts might go yellow and brown, but surely they would rot and fall apart before going black!

The belt system was in fact taken from judo in the 1920s by Gichin Funakoshi. It was therefore actually invented by Jigoru Kano. Originally, judo only had two belt colors, white and black, but Kano introduced a belt above black belt to recognize high-ranking black belts. This was made up of alternating red and white panels and was awarded to sixth-, seventh- and eighth-degree grades. This innovation was made after Funakoshi had adopted the belt system, so it was not reflected in the karate belt tradition.

Funakoshi awarded the first shodan ranks given in karate to Tokuda, Otsuka, Akiba, Shimizu, Hirose, Gima, and Kasuya on April 10, 1924.

In most organizations, there are 10 dan grades, from first-degree black belt up to tenth-degree black belt, which is usually held by the head of the organization. However, many organizations do not use this many grades in their system, nor is there an upper limit on the number of dan grades that a system might use. Some organizations, for example the shotokai associations, limit the black belt grades to a maximum of fifth dan.

The first few dan grades are awarded based on physical ability and usually require attending a grading examination in the same way as for previous grades. The higher dan grades are awarded based more on teaching experience, leadership ability, service to the organization and tenure.

Grading Examinations

In order to progress from one karate rank to another and to get your next belt, you will need to take a grading examination (commonly just called 'gradings'). Typically, there should be a minimum of three months between each grading, but this will depend on how much training you put in during that period.

Do not consider rank as something to use to measure yourself against others. Everyone is different. You should compete against yourself and not the person standing next to you in line. Gradings are cumulative: you need to know everything from previous gradings. Rank is not about how good a fighter you are. You are not required to be able to 'defeat' anyone to achieve your rank.

GRADING TIPS

- Do not hold back at the grading. Give it everything you've got.

- Even if you make a mistake, keep going. Do not highlight the mistake by showing an emotional response to it.

- Relax. Worrying won't help. A major rationale behind the grading is to see how you cope under stressful situations.

The grading examiner will use the following criteria to judge your performance:

KEY GRADING REQUIREMENTS	
Correct form	Correct stance and hand positions.
Power and speed	Techniques should be explosive (using kime).
Attitude	Eyes should be focused ahead, not at the ground. Techniques should be confident and vigorous. Use a strong kiai on the last technique in a sequence when performing kihon.
Timing	Hands and feet should finish at the same time. When sparring, do not start blocking before the technique gets near you. On the other hand, don't leave it so late that you get hit.
Distancing	Execute techniques to the optimal distance. Don't overreach or try blocking too near to your own body. Be aware of your natural comfortable range (know how long your arm is). When sparring, make sure your attack reaches your partner but is focused so that they are not hurt.

CHAPTER **THREE** beginner to orange belt

Getting started is the most difficult part of karate training for most people. Karate classes often train all levels of students together, and for the beginner, this can be quite daunting. However, you should see this as an opportunity to see skills further down the line and to gauge what you may expect your ability level to be after various amounts of training.

As a beginner, the most difficult skills to learn will seem to be coordination between the arms and legs and general spatial awareness. These alone can deter beginners from continuing their training.

Beginners should not expect too much too quickly. It can take several hours of training to get comfortable with the coordination. Karate training consists of repetitive exercises that, through long-term dedication, teach the body new reflex actions.

For the first grading, all the blocking and punching techniques are also stepping techniques. One hand technique corresponds to one step. So, if you step forward with the left foot, you should be doing a block or punch with the left hand.

Syllabus Summary

White belt gradings follow the following format:

WHITE BELT GRADING SYLLABUS	
Basics	
Stepping punch	Oi-zuki
Rising block	Age-uke
Outside block	Soto-uke
Inside block	Uchi-uke
Front kick	Mae-geri
Kata	
Kihon Kata (Taikyoku Shodan)	
Kumite	
Five-step sparring	Gohon kumite

Basic Form

NATURAL STANCES

Shizen-tai

The natural stances are so called because they are all variations on how you would stand naturally. They require no tension in the legs and have the weight distributed evenly between the feet.

In the formal attention stance, heisoku-dachi (literally translated as 'closed feet stance'), the feet are together with the heels and big toes just touching.

In the informal attention stance, musubi-dachi (literally translated as 'connected stance'), the heels touch, but the feet point out diagonally in a 'V' shape.

In the parallel-feet stance, heiko-dachi, the feet are parallel and one shoulder-width apart.

Shizen-tai literally means 'natural body.' If your karate instructor says 'Shizen-tai,' he wants you to stand in heiko-dachi, with your arms straight and your hands making fists held just in front of you at hip height. This is also called ready stance, yoi-dachi.

Heisoku-dachi

Musubi-dachi

Heiko-dachi

FRONT STANCE

Zenkutsu-dachi

Front stance is used for lunging attacks. There should be no more than one hip-width between the axis of the front foot and the rear heel. The stance should be at least two hip-widths long, preferably longer. Make sure that the front leg is bent sufficiently with about 60 percent of your body weight over the front leg. You should not be able to see your toes because they should be obscured by your front knee.

Long, low stances are characteristic of shotokan karate. A deep front stance is difficult to maintain, but it helps with the development of both leg strength and flexibility. It offers good balance and stability, but this is traded off against speed and mobility. At a higher level, you will learn to mitigate these drawbacks by using the front stance as a transitional position, holding it only for an instant before moving on to a higher, more dynamic stance. You should use as low and long a stance as you can when practicing the basic techniques in kihon, kata and kumite.

Front stance, zenkutsu-dachi

There are two hip positions that can be used when in front stance:

- The full front-facing hips position is achieved by pushing the hip forward with the back leg. In this position, the back knee must be straight.

- The half front-facing hips position involves pulling one hip back so that the chest faces 45 degrees to the side. In this position, the back knee will be slightly bent.

When moving in front stance, consider the following points:

- Move in a sliding motion while stepping with the feet touching the ground throughout, even if it is only a light pressure. Keep the heel down on the front foot.

- Do not allow your hips to bob up and down. Your hips should be driven forward in a straight line parallel with the floor.

- Keep your back and neck upright but in a natural posture, which is to say that your back should not be as straight as a board. Leaning very slightly forward is natural and preferable as a fighting posture. Leaning backward is a big mistake.

- Keep your knees pointing in the same direction as your feet. To do otherwise puts unnecessary stress on the ankles and could result in an injury.

- In front stance, your front foot should point forward. When stepping forward, this foot will twist out to the side as you finish the step, but make sure that this happens as late as possible into the step. A common error is to allow this to happen as the first action before stepping.

MAKING A FIST

Before you can punch or block, you need to make a fist. It is important to get this right or you could end up hurting your hands on impact.

It is important to keep the fist tight on impact because this offers protection to the fingers. Almost all karate techniques demand that you keep the wrist straight. This is especially important when punching.

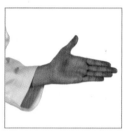

1

Start with your hands open.

2

Starting with the fourth finger and finishing with the index finger, close the middle and top finger joints so that the fingertips touch the top of the palm at the base of the finger.

3

Continue to fold the fingers in tightly.

4

Fold the thumb in so that it touches the second (middle) phalanx of the index and second finger.

DOWNWARD BLOCK

Gedan Barai

Gedan barai (literal translation 'lower-level sweep') is a downward block that can be used to defend against low-level attacks, deflecting them to the side. It is one of the most versatile moves in karate and can be used not just for deflecting incoming punches and kicks but also as an attack itself. It is usual in a karate class for gedan barai to be used every time you step forward ready to practice basic form. Your instructor will say something like, 'Step forward, gedan barai.' This technique is also often used on turns when you are standing in front stance. The instructor will say 'mawatte,' which means 'turn around.'

In gedan barai, the opposite hip is pulled away from the block so that your hips and chest face to the side. This contrasts with the action used with the stepping punch, which is described in the next section. Ensure that you are still looking forward and that your front foot and knee point forward.

The opposite hand is pulled back to the hip so that it is on, or just above, the belt. This is known as hikite, meaning 'pulling hand.' This pulling action should be as strong as the blocking technique. Almost every time you do a technique in karate, you will have to use hikite, and a common mistake is to have a weak hikite or to leave it out altogether.

1

Start in ready stance.

2

Prepare to block with the left arm.

3

Block to the lower level by sweeping the left arm down across the body.

STEPPING PUNCH

Oi-zuki

The stepping punch (or 'chasing punch,' which is the literal translation of oi-zuki) is a lunging attack used to cover a big distance. Power is generated mainly from the step, so body weight must be put behind the punch. The punching hand should move in a straight line from the hip to the target and should be angled in slightly so that it hits in line with the center of the body. On completion of the technique, ensure that your hips and chest are squarely pointing forward and that the rear leg is straight.

1

Start in front stance, zenkutsu-dachi.

2

Bring the knees together. Start to punch and withdraw the other hand.

3

Step forward into zenkutsu-dachi and finish the punch at the same time. Rotate the fist at the end of the punching action.

Here are some training tips to help you punch correctly:

- Keep your elbows close to your body and behind the punch.
- Punch straight, with the fist traveling in a straight line from the hip to the target.
- The fist of the punching hand should stay palm-up throughout the punch and then rotate at the end.
- Strongly pull the opposite hand (hikite) in the same way as with the downward block.
- Relax unnecessary muscles. Do not hunch the shoulders.

INSIDE BLOCK

Uchi-uke

The blocking arm sweeps across the body and can be used to defend against stomach-level attacks, deflecting them to the side. The fist starts palm side down in the preparation. It then rotates so that it is facing toward you at the end of the block. The blocking hand should move on the outside of the retracting hand. As you block, pull back the opposite hip and hand so that your chest faces to the side and your retracting hand finishes on your hip. The blocking arm finishes so that it is bent at 90 degrees, with the fist in line with the shoulder.

1

Start in front stance, zenkutsu-dachi.

2

Prepare to block with the left arm.

3

Step forward and block with the left arm.

OUTSIDE BLOCK

Soto-uke

This block sweeps from head level down across the body and can be used to defend against stomach-level attacks, deflecting them to the side. The fist starts palm side facing away from you in the preparation and rotates so that it is facing toward you at the end of the block. As you block, pull back the opposite hip and hand so that your chest faces to the side and your retracting hand finishes on your hip. The blocking arm finishes so that it is bent 90 degrees, with the fist in line with the shoulder. This is the same finish position as with the inside block.

1

Start in front stance, zenkutsu-dachi.

2

Prepare to block with the right arm.

3

Step forward and block with the right arm.

RISING BLOCK

Age-uke

The rising block can be used to defend against head-level attacks, deflecting them up over your head. The blocking fist should move up the centerline of the body, as if doing an uppercut. The blocking hand should move on the outside of the retracting hand and should be rotated at the end of the block so that the palm is facing away from the head. As you block, pull back the opposite hip and hand so that your chest faces to the side and your retracting hand finishes on your hip.

1

Start in front stance, zenkutsu-dachi.

2

Prepare to block with the right arm.

3

Step forward and block with the right arm.

FRONT KICK
Mae-geri

Try to lift the knee of the kicking leg as high as possible in preparation for the kick, but ensure that your body does not rise up. This can be achieved by aiming to drop your body weight while raising the knee.

1

Start in front stance, zenkutsu-dachi, with your arms out to the sides.

2

Raise the knee.

3

Kick. Strike with the ball of the foot.

4

Snap back before stepping forward.

REVERSE PUNCH

Gyaku-zuki

The reverse punch is the most commonly used counterattack. It is very popular in sports karate, and most scoring techniques in karate tournaments are with the reverse punch. The hips are thrown toward the target just ahead of the punch. Be careful not to overreach by bending your back. Keep upright throughout the technique, doing the work with the legs and hips. Remember to follow the same punching form as for stepping punch.

1

Start from front stance with the right hip and fist pulled back.

2

Punch with the right hand by throwing the right hip and chest forward.

Kihon Kata

Gichin Funakoshi created three Taikyoku kata: Taikyoku Shodan, Taikyoku Nidan and Taikyoku Sandan. In general, the latter two kata are not taught by shotokan schools but are typically practiced in shotokai schools. The first kata you will learn is Taikyoku Shodan. It acts as an introduction to kata before starting on the more sophisticated Heian kata. This kata is often called Kihon Kata (meaning basic kata) by shotokan schools.

TRAINING TIP

In Kihon Kata, there are only two hand movements: downward blocks and punches. Ensure that these two moves are distinct. A downward block follows a curved path and finishes at low level. A punch follows a straight path and, in the kata, finishes at stomach level (ideally at the height of the solar plexus, but at the very least ensure that it is lower than your shoulder and higher than your hip).

STARTING AND FINISHING THE KATA

Kihon Kata (and all the Heian kata) start and finish in the same manner. The procedure for starting and finishing is as much a part of a complete kata performance as any of the actual techniques of the kata.

When finishing, hold the last position until told to relax. Then bow to finish.

1

Start in ready stance, yoi-dachi.

2

Put the feet together in mosubo-dachi. Bow and announce your kata in a loud and confident manner.

3

Step into ready stance.

KATA SEQUENCE

Bow. Announce kata 'Kihon' and step into ready stance, yoi-dachi.

1

Step to the left and downward block, gedan barai, to the left.

2

Stepping punch with the right hand.

3

Move the right foot to turn 180 degrees and execute right-side downward block.

4

Stepping punch with the left hand.

5

Step to the left and downward block, gedan barai, to the left.

6

Step forward and punch with the right hand.

7

Step forward and punch with the left hand.

8

Step forward and punch with the right hand. Kiai.

9

Move the left foot to turn 270 degrees and execute left-side downward block, gedan barai.

10

Step forward and punch with the right hand.

11

Move the right foot to turn 180 degrees and execute right-side downward block, gedan barai.

12

Step forward and punch with the left hand.

13

Step to the left and downward block, gedan barai, to the left.

14

Step forward and punch with the right hand.

15

Step forward and punch with the left hand.

16

Step forward and punch with the right hand. Kiai.

17

Move the left foot to turn 270 degrees and execute left-side downward block, gedan barai.

18

Step forward and punch with the right hand.

19

Move the right foot to turn 180 degrees and execute right-side downward block, gedan barai.

20

Step forward and punch with the left hand.

Move the left foot back into ready position and finish with a bow.

KATA APPLICATION

Karate kata contain within them highly effective self-defense moves. These kata applications are very dangerous if performed correctly. The applications presented here are intended to illustrate the correct performance and uses of the kata. If you practice these applications with a partner, it should be done with extreme care so as to ensure that you do not cause an injury. For this reason, it is highly recommended that you practice kata applications at slow speed.

This is an example application of the first two moves in Kihon Kata.

1

The attacker starts in front stance with the left leg forward. The attacker steps and punches with his right hand. The defender deflects the punch with his left hand while simultaneously attacking with a low punch using the right hand.

2

The defender steps alongside and attacks the groin with his left hand.

3

The defender steps past the attacker with his right foot and uses his right arm and hip to throw his opponent.

Sparring Forms

Kumite

Sparring (kumite) is an exercise performed between two karate practitioners where the objective is to work together to improve technique, targeting, distancing and timing. The objective is *not* to injure your partner, nor is it to 'win' a fight.

There are many variants of kumite. At the beginner level, it takes the form of five-step sparring, gohon kumite, where all the attacks, blocks and counters are prearranged. The example below shows one-step sparring, ippon kumite. In five-step sparring, step 2 is repeated a further four times and a kiai is added to the last punch only.

BOWING

Before you start sparring, bow to your partner. This shows respect and is a signal to say that you are now ready. When you have finished the sparring sequence, bow again. This again shows respect but also is a signal that you are finished and do not expect any more attacks!

HEAD-LEVEL (JODAN) ATTACK

1

Both the attacker and the defender start in ready position. The attacker steps back with a downward block and announces the attack: 'Jodan!'

2

The attacker steps forward and punches, targeting the head. The defender steps back and blocks with a rising block. This is repeated four more times during five-step sparring (but only kiai on the fifth attack).

3

The defender counterattacks using reverse punch with kiai. The punch should be focused so that it just makes contact. It should not hurt your opponent but must not fall short. The attacker withdraws, and as he does so, the defender steps up, both finishing in ready stance, yoi-dachi.

STOMACH-LEVEL (CHUDAN) ATTACK

1

Both the attacker and the defender start in ready position. The attacker steps back with a downward block and announces the attack: 'Chudan!'

2

The attacker steps forward and punches, targeting the body. The defender steps back and blocks with an outside block. This is repeated four more times in five-step sparring (but only using kiai on the fifth attack).

3

The defender counterattacks using a reverse punch with kiai. The punch should be focused so that it just makes contact. It should not hurt your opponent but must not fall short. The attacker withdraws, and as he does so, the defender steps up, both finishing in ready stance, yoi-dachi.

IMPORTANCE OF FIVE-STEP SPARRING

Although five-step sparring seems simple, it has benefits for all levels. It helps develop a committed attitude to attacking and defending and helps with targeting and distancing skills.

Because there are five steps, any mistakes in the first step will be amplified in the following ones, something that will not happen in one-step sparring. If the defender is not stepping back far enough on each step, then by the fourth and fifth steps they will find the attacker right on top of them and so will find it increasingly difficult to block effectively.

Ensure that you still use correct form to execute your techniques. This means using full preparations for the blocks, pulling back the reverse hand on punches and using correct stances.

TARGETING

Ensure that your attacks are on target. If you don't, there will be no reason for your training partner to block. If you and your sparring partner tend to punch off target, then your blocking techniques will not have an opportunity to develop. When doing gohon kumite, your target areas should be those that are safest for your sparring partner. For jodan attacks, target the chin. For chudan attacks, target the stomach.

DISTANCING

You must ensure that you make the correct distance when punching. This is particularly important when counterattacking. With correct distancing, you should make contact with your target, but in order that you do not hurt your sparring partner, you should focus the attack on the target's surface.

If you find that you are too far away from your partner after you have blocked, you need to make more distance when counterattacking. Do this by pushing in your hip and bending your front leg. If this is insufficient, you will have to shuffle in as you punch.

COMMON MISTAKES

Overreaching

Don't try to extend your range by leaning forward. This will unbalance you so that the next step will be harder. It will also move your head nearer to your opponent, which in general is a bad idea while sparring. If you need to make more distance, do it using your legs, either by making a longer and deeper stance or by shuffling your feet nearer.

Leaning Forward When Blocking

Although this may feel like you're moving your stomach and groin out of range, you're actually moving your chest and face *into* range of the attack. In five-step sparring, you will find it harder to escape the next attack if you lean forward on the block. If the attacker's punch is far away, do not feel that you have to lean forward so that your block can reach. If the punch cannot reach you, don't worry about it. You do not need to block an attack that cannot hit you.

Incorrect form: attacker leaning into the attack

Incorrect form: defender leaning forward

Maintaining Front Stance

Make sure that you use correct stances. A common mistake is failing to bend the front leg. This will make it harder to make the correct distance to your target when you punch.

Incorrect form: attacker not bending the front leg

Attitude and Kiai

Do not underestimate the importance of a strong attitude. Without a strong attitude, your attacks will not be effective. Use a strong kiai to demonstrate good spirit and strengthen your resolve.

CHAPTER **FOUR** orange to red belt

The primary challenge faced at orange belt is learning the side kicks. For many students, these physically demanding kicks are not mastered until a much higher level. The orange belt level also introduces the knife-hand block, which is a key technique in shotokan karate, one that is often pivotal in kata performances.

Syllabus Summary

Orange belt gradings follow the following format:

ORANGE BELT GRADING SYLLABUS	
Basics	
Stepping punch	Oi-zuki
Rising block	Age-uke
Outside block	Soto-uke
Inside block	Uchi-uke
Knife-hand block	Shuto-uke
Front kick	Mae-geri
Side thrusting kick	Yoko kekomi
Side rising kick	Yoko keage
Kata	
Heian Shodan	
Kumite	
Five-step sparring	Gohon kumite

Basic Form

SIDE STANCE
Kiba-dachi

In this stance, the feet are placed about two shoulder-widths apart, with the feet parallel and facing forward. The weight must be evenly spread between the feet. Bend the knees and maintain an outward tension, pulling the knees outward. Kiba-dachi is good for developing both leg flexibility and strength and is also useful for close-range attacking and throwing. As with the front stance, keep your back and neck straight.

Side stance, kiba-dachi

BACK STANCE

Kokutsu-dachi

In this stance, the feet are placed two shoulder-widths apart, with the feet perpendicular to each other. The front foot should be facing forward and the back foot facing to the side. Most of the weight (about 70 percent) should be on the back foot. Bend the back leg, lowering the stance to the same height as in front stance. The front leg should be slightly bent, and the back should be straight and upright.

How to step forward when in back stance:

1

Start in back stance.

2

Bring the knees together. Try to keep your hips at the same height.

3

Push the right foot forward, keeping all the weight on the left foot.

4

Step forward into back stance by abruptly rotating the hips and pushing the right foot forward.

KNIFE-HAND BLOCK
Shuto-uke

This technique uses the outside fleshy part of the hand to block. It can also be used as a striking technique at close range against the neck. Unlike the other techniques, the retracting hand remains open and pulls back to protect the solar plexus, which is the soft spot along the centerline of the body just below the ribs.

1

Start in ready stance.

2

Prepare to block with the left arm by bringing it up to the shoulder with the palm facing toward the ear. Reach forward with the other hand, palm down.

3

Execute shuto-uke to stomach level and step into back stance.

Training Tips

- Pull the elbow of the blocking hand in close to your centerline.
- Try to time the blocking action to coincide with the twisting of your hips as you settle into back stance.
- Keep your hands tense with your fingers together.

HAMMER-HAND STRIKE
Tetsui-uchi

This strike is done with the fleshy underside of the fist and can be used to attack the collarbone or the nose.

1

Start in front stance with gedan barai.

2

Pull back the leading hand using the whole body.

3

Swing the fist up over your head.

4

Strike with the base of the fist at collarbone height.

Training Tips

- Make the arm and foot movements big, but don't pull your body weight back too far as it will slow down the subsequent forward motion.
- Finish with the elbow at 90 degrees.

SIDE RISING KICK
Yoko Keage

This kick is also known as side snap kick because, after the kick, the foot is pulled back in a whipping action. The direction of the kick is upward and can be targeted at the chin or armpit. The striking surface is the edge of the foot, not the toes, sole or heel.

1

Start in side stance, kiba-dachi.

2

Step forward with the right foot.

3

Lift the left knee so that it is pointing to the side.

4

Kick to the side. Use your hip to throw the kick. Rotate the supporting foot on the ball of the foot.

5

Snap back.

6

Step down into side stance.

SIDE THRUSTING KICK

Yoko Kekomi

Ensure that the knee lift before the kick is high. Try to make the kicking foot go in a straight line to the target from this preparation position. Do not allow the kicking foot to drop down below the level you are kicking to. At the point of maximum extension, lock the kick in position because this is a thrust kick. The striking area is the heel of the foot, with the foot pointing diagonally downward. Make sure that you bring the leg back to the recoil position (as shown in step 5) before stepping down: do not let the leg just drop to the floor after kicking.

1

Start in side stance, kiba-dachi.

2

Step forward with the right foot.

3

Lift the left knee so that it is pointing to the front.

4

Kick to the side and hold briefly. Ensure that the supporting leg is bent. Feel like you are pushing your whole body weight into the target.

5

Pull the kicking leg back into the same position as in step 3.

6

Step down into side stance.

Heian Shodan

This is the first in the Heian series of kata. Heian simply translated means 'peace.' The Heian kata were created by Master Itosu at the beginning of the 20th century. They were originally called the Pinan kata in Okinawa and were renamed in Japanese as part of the 'Japanification' of karate by Gichin Funakoshi. He also reordered the kata: the shotokan kata we today call Heian Shodan was originally the second in the Heian series of kata, but Funakoshi presumably realized that the kata that was originally first in the series was much harder. Other styles of karate, such as wado-ryu, call this kata by the original name of Pinan Nidan.

KATA SEQUENCE

Bow. Announce kata 'Heian Shodan' and step into ready stance, yoi-dachi.

1

Step to the left and downward block, gedan barai, to the left.

2

Stepping punch with the right hand.

3

Move the right foot to turn 180 degrees and execute right-side downward block.

4

Execute hammer-hand strike on the spot.

5

Stepping punch with the left hand.

6

Step to the left and downward block, gedan barai, to the left.

7

Step forward and execute right rising block, age-uke.

8

Step forward and execute left rising block, age-uke.

9

Step forward and execute right rising block, age-uke. Kiai.

10

Move the left foot to turn 270 degrees and execute left-side downward block.

11

Step forward and punch with the right hand.

12

Move the right leg to turn 180 degrees and execute right-side downward block.

13

Step forward and punch with the left hand.

14

Step to the left and downward block, gedan barai, to the left.

15

Step forward and punch with the right hand.

16

Step forward and punch with the left hand.

17

Step forward and punch with the right hand. Kiai.

18

Move the left foot to turn 270 degrees and execute left-side knife-hand block.

19

Step forward at 45 degrees with a right-side knife-hand block.

20

Pivot on your left foot for 135 degrees and execute right-side knife-hand block.

21

Step forward at 45 degrees with a left-side knife-hand block.

Finish by moving the left foot back into ready stance and bowing.

KATA APPLICATION

This is a possible application of the hammer-hand strike (move 4) in Heian Shodan.

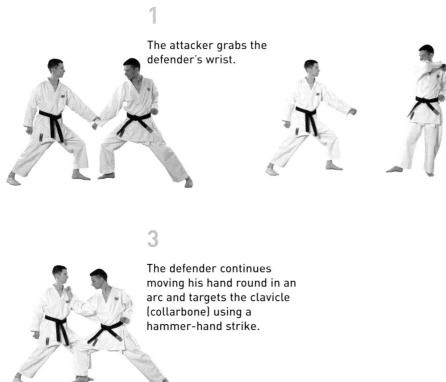

1

The attacker grabs the defender's wrist.

2

The defender pulls back his leading arm, using his body weight in order to break out of the grab.

3

The defender continues moving his hand round in an arc and targets the clavicle (collarbone) using a hammer-hand strike.

CHAPTER **FIVE** red to yellow belt

The red belt syllabus introduces the concept of attacking and defending with combinations of techniques, where one technique follows another. This can be a challenge of coordination at first, with students sometimes finding it hard to decide which hand to use next, but any difficulty is ultimately overcome by repetition of the combinations.

Syllabus Summary

Red belt gradings follow the following format:

RED BELT GRADING SYLLABUS	
Basics	
Triple punch	Sanbon tsuki
Rising block, reverse punch	Age-uke, gyaku-zuki
Outside block, reverse punch	Soto-uke, gyaku-zuki
Inside block, reverse punch	Uchi-uke, gyaku-zuki
Knife-hand block	Shuto-uke
Front kick	Mae-geri
Side thrusting kick	Yoko kekomi
Side rising kick	Yoko keage
Kata	
Heian Nidan	
Kumite	
Five-step sparring	Gohon kumite

Basic Form

TRIPLE PUNCH
Sanbon tsuki

This combination consists of a stepping punch followed immediately by two punches on the spot. Ensure that all the punches are lined up with the center of your body. Each time you punch, make sure you retract the other hand back to the hip.

1

Start in front stance.

2

Step forward and punch to head level, jodan oi-zuki.

3

Without stepping, reverse punch to stomach level, chudan gyaku-zuki, using the left hand.

4

Punch the right hand to stomach level.

RISING BLOCK, REVERSE PUNCH

Age-uke, Gyaku-zuki

Ensure that you pull back the hip on the block and push the hip forward on the reverse punch.

1

Start in front stance.

2

Step forward and block to head level with rising block, age-uke.

3

Without stepping, reverse punch with the left hand to stomach level, chudan gyaku-zuki.

57

OUTSIDE BLOCK, REVERSE PUNCH
Soto-uke, Gyaku-zuki
Ensure that you pull back the hip on the block and push the hip forward on the reverse punch.

1

Start in front stance.

2

Step forward and block to stomach level with outside block, soto-uke.

3

Without stepping, reverse punch with the left hand to stomach level, chudan gyaku-zuki.

INSIDE BLOCK, REVERSE PUNCH
Uchi-uke, Gyaku-zuki

Ensure that you pull back the hip on the block and push the hip forward on the reverse punch.

1

Start in front stance.

2

Step forward and block to stomach level with inside block, uchi-uke.

3

Without stepping, reverse punch with the left hand to stomach level, chudan gyaku-zuki.

DOUBLE-HANDED BLOCK
Morote-uke

This is the same as an inside block except that the blocking fist is followed by the other fist, which should finish by pushing just below the blocking elbow. It is often called an augmented or reinforced block, but this is misleading because the second hand does not actually augment the block. The term morote just means that both hands are used. When morote-uke is used in kata, it is often actually a throw or an arm lock.

1

Start in front stance.

2

Prepare by pulling both hands to the right hip.

3

Step into front stance while simultaneously blocking with the left hand and pushing with the right fist just below the elbow.

SPEAR-HAND STRIKE

Nukite-uchi

The spear-hand strike is made by pointing the fingers and striking with the fingertips. This strike is effective when used against small, soft targets like the throat or the solar plexus. The fingers should be kept tense and together. The striking hand should move in a straight line to the target and should be angled in slightly (just like a stepping punch) so that it hits in line with the center of the body. In Heian Nidan, you practice the spear-hand strike in combination with a blocking motion so that the left hand finishes palm down under the right elbow.

1

Start in back stance.

2

Step into front stance while simultaneously blocking with the left hand, palm down, and striking with the right-hand fingertips to stomach level.

BACK-FIST STRIKE
Uraken-uchi
This technique is made by striking with the first two knuckles on the top of the fist. It should be done using a whipping action. This is one technique in karate where bending the wrist is necessary because this allows you to hit with the knuckles, rather than the fragile small bones on the back of the hand.

1

Start in front stance.

2

Prepare to strike with the left arm. Point the left elbow at the target.

3

Step into front stance while simultaneously striking with the back of the fist to head level.

4

Snap back the attack.

HAMMER-HAND STRIKE

Tetsui-uchi

This technique can also be called the bottom-fist strike because it is done by striking with the bottom of the fist.

1

Start in front stance.

2

Prepare to strike with the left arm. Point the left elbow at the target.

3

Step into side stance while simultaneously striking with the bottom of the fist to chest level.

63

STRIKING AREAS
Make sure that you use the correct area of the hand when employing the different strikes.

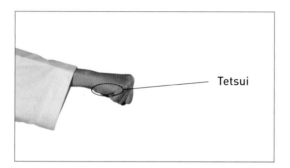 Tetsui

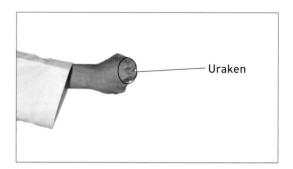 Uraken

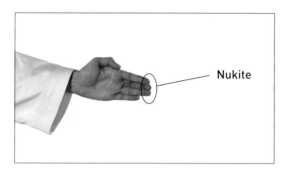 Nukite

Heian Nidan

This is the second kata in the Heian series of kata. Heian Nidan makes extensive use of back stance and knife-hand block. In fact, except for one technique, the first 16 moves are all performed in back stance. To perform this kata well, it is therefore imperative to ensure that your back stance is well-formed, as described in the previous chapter.

KATA SEQUENCE

Bow. Announce kata 'Heian Nidan' and step into ready stance, yoi-dachi.

1

Step with the left foot into back stance. Block the upper level to the side with the left arm and above the forehead with the right arm.

2

Block with the left arm and strike with the right arm.

3

Hammer-hand strike sideways with the left arm.

4

Pivot to face the other way and block the upper level to the side with the right arm and above the forehead with the left arm.

5

Block with the right arm and strike with the left arm.

6

Hammer-hand strike sideways with the right arm.

7

Shift the left foot to the center and lift the right foot to the left knee. Place both fists on the left hip.

8

Side rising kick with the right leg and back-fist strike with the right hand.

8

Side view.

9

Step down with the right foot into back stance with knife-hand block.

10

Step forward with right-hand knife-hand block.

11

Step forward with left-hand knife-hand block.

12

Block down with the left hand, palm down. Strike with a spear-hand, nukite, over the top with the right hand. Kiai.

13

Move the left foot and turn into back stance with left-hand knife-hand block.

14

Step forward, with the right foot at an angle of 45 degrees, into back stance with right-hand knife-hand block.

15

Move the right foot across into back stance with right-hand knife-hand block.

16

Step with the left foot at an angle of 45 degrees into back stance with left-hand knife-hand block.

17

Move the left foot across and block with right-hand inside block.

17

Side view.

18

Without changing arm positions, front kick with the right leg.

18

Side view.

67

19

Step into front stance and punch with the left hand.

19

Side view.

20

Without stepping, execute inside block with the left hand.

20

Side view.

21

Without changing arm positions, front kick with the left leg.

21

Side view.

22

Step into front stance and punch with the right hand.

22

Side view.

23

Step forward into front stance and block with right-side morote-uke.

23

Side view.

24

Turn 270 degrees by moving the left foot and execute left downward block.

25

Step using the right foot at an angle of 45 degrees and execute right rising block.

26

Turn 135 degrees by moving the right foot and execute right downward block.

27

Step using the left leg at an angle of 45 degrees and execute left rising block with kiai.

Finish by moving the left foot back into ready stance and bowing.

KATA APPLICATION

This is a simple application of moves 1, 2 and 3 in Heian Nidan that will help in developing these techniques.

1

The attacker prepares to attack with a hook punch.

2

The defender blocks using head-level inside block, jodan uchi-uke.

3

The attacker punches with his left fist. The defender blocks across the face, nagashi-uke, with his left arm and strikes the attacker's elbow with his right arm, tetsui-uchi.

4

The defender counters by striking to the head with the left fist.

CHAPTER **SIX** yellow to green belt

At yellow belt level, you will be expected to be able to switch smoothly between different types of stance. It is therefore important to understand the differences between the major stances, zenkutsu, kokutsu and kiba-dachi. A common mistake is to fail to distinguish between the stances and to end up using some sort of hybrid stance throughout the yellow belt combinations or sections of the kata.

Syllabus Summary

Yellow belt gradings follow the following format:

YELLOW BELT GRADING SYLLABUS	
Basics	
Triple punch	Sanbon tsuki
Rising block, reverse punch, downward block	Age-uke, gyaku-zuki, gedan barai
Outside block, elbow strike	Soto-uke, empi-uchi
Inside block, reverse punch	Uchi-uke, gyaku-zuki
Knife-hand block, spear-hand strike	Shuto-uke, nukite
Consecutive front kicks	Mae ren-geri
Side thrusting kick	Yoko kekomi
Side rising kick	Yoko keage
Kata	
Heian Sandan	
Kumite	
One-step sparring	Ippon kumite
Head-level stepping punch	Jodan oi-zuki
Stomach-level stepping punch	Chudan oi-zuki

Basic Form

RISING BLOCK, REVERSE PUNCH, DOWNWARD BLOCK
Age-uke, Gyaku-zuki, Gedan Barai

Ensure that you pull back the opposite hip on the block and push that hip forward on the reverse punch. The hips should then be pulled back again on the final block. Try to make the first punch follow on quickly from the rising block and then leave a brief pause before the final block. The timing should then be block, punch, pause, block.

Make sure that every individual technique is completed: do not make the rising block smaller in order to get to the punch more quickly. Every individual technique should be done at the same speed. (Do not confuse this with the timing, which is concerned with the spaces between individual techniques rather than the techniques themselves.) A common mistake is to execute the first two techniques vigorously but then to move the hands slowly for the last block.

1
Start in front stance, zenkutsu-dachi.

2
Step forward and block to head level with rising block, age-uke.

3
Without stepping, reverse punch with the left hand to stomach level, chudan gyaku-zuki.

4
Without stepping, block to right-hand lower sweeping block, gedan barai.

OUTSIDE BLOCK, ELBOW STRIKE

Soto-uke, Empi-uchi

Make sure that when you block, you are in front stance with the opposite hip pulled back. Use a big preparation for the elbow strike. When pulling back the front leg for the elbow strike preparation, ensure your movements remain dynamic by leaving your balance slightly forward. This means you can drive forward into the strike.

Do not make the mistake of merging the blocking action and the elbow striking action: there should be a distinct block in a good front stance.

1

Start in front stance, zenkutsu-dachi.

2

Step forward into front stance, zenkutsu-dachi, and block to stomach level with outside block, soto-uke.

3

Slide the right foot back and prepare to strike by pulling the right hand back. Reach forward with the left hand.

4

Slide the right foot forward into side stance, kiba-dachi, and simultaneously execute right arm elbow strike, empi-uchi.

75

KNIFE-HAND BLOCK, SPEAR-HAND STRIKE
Shuto-uke, Nukite-uchi

Make sure that you step into back stance for the knife-hand block and then shift your weight forward into front stance for the spear-hand strike. You should complete the block before moving for the counterattack. A common mistake is to merge the two techniques, resulting in a weak block.

The retracted hand should remain open and finish on the solar plexus for the knife-hand block. For the spear-hand strike, your retracting hand should close into a fist and finish on the hip.

1

Start in back stance.

2

Step into back stance while simultaneously blocking with knife-hand block, shuto-uke.

3

Without stepping, push the right hip forward into front stance and execute spear-hand strike, nukite-uchi, with the right hand.

CONSECUTIVE FRONT KICKS

Mae Ren-geri

The two kicks in mae ren-geri should be done in quick succession (in 'one breath'). Do not pause or even step into stance after the first kick. Both kicks are intended to be aimed at the same opponent, so be aware of the range of the two kicks. The first kick, which is a long-reaching kick, is to stomach level. The step after this should be very short (step down just in front of the supporting foot) so that the head-level kick, which is a short-range kick, reaches no further than the first.

1

Start in front stance.

2

Front kick with the left leg to stomach level, chudan mae-geri.

3

Step down in a short stance.

4

Immediately kick with the right leg to head level, jodan mae-geri.

DOUBLE CROSSING BLOCK

This is the technique that characterizes the kata Heian Sandan (moves 2, 3, 5 and 6). It is more of a lock than a block, but it is simpler to think of this at first as a blocking technique. The key to doing this technique well is to fold your arms so that your elbows are tight together and then to unfold your arms explosively. It will feel like your arms are going to collide, but don't worry – they won't. Try to make the movements as big and as bold as possible, blocking right across your body. Don't make the common mistake of simply waving your arms up and down without the folding action.

1

Start in ready stance.

2

Prepare by bringing the right arm alongside the left shoulder and reach forward and down with the left arm, bringing the elbows together.

3

Downward block, gedan barai, with the right arm and inside block, uchi-uke, with the left arm. Try to get your arms to cross close together, with the downward block passing closer to your body than the inside block.

4

Now repeat: fold and unfold your arms. Imagine that someone has grabbed your left arm and that your right arm will knock their arm to your right and break their grip.

Heian Sandan

This is the third kata in the Heian series of kata. It contains examples of the yellow belt theme of switching between different stances. Attention must also be paid to this kata's signature moves: the double crossing block and the knee lifts. Heian Sandan is the first kata to make use of a sliding foot technique (yori-ashi), and this occurs in the last two moves of the kata.

KATA SEQUENCE

Bow. Announce kata 'Heian Sandan' and step into ready stance, yoi-dachi.

1

Step with the left foot into back stance. Block to stomach level with inside block to the left.

2a

Move the right foot up to the left foot and prepare by crossing the right arm to the left hip and the left arm to the right shoulder.

2b

Straighten the legs and at the same time cross and uncross the arms, blocking inside block with the right arm and downward block with the left arm.

3

Cross and uncross the arms, blocking inside block with the left arm and downward block with the right arm.

4

Step with the right foot so you face the other way and block to stomach level with inside block to the side with the right arm.

5a

Move the left foot up to the right foot and prepare by crossing the left hand to the right hip and the right hand to the left shoulder.

5b

Straighten the legs and at the same time cross and uncross the arms, blocking inside block with the left arm and downward block with the right arm.

6

Cross and uncross the arms, blocking inside block with the right arm and downward block with the left arm.

7

Step with the left foot into back stance and use double-handed morote-uke.

8

Block palm-down with the left hand and strike over the top with spear-hand strike.

9

Move the left foot, rotating the body anticlockwise, and strike hammer-hand, tetsui-uchi, with the left hand.

10

Step forward and punch with the right hand. Kiai.

11

Slowly, and with control, move the left foot toward the right into heisoku-dachi and rotate the body anticlockwise 180 degrees.

12

Lift the right knee.

12

Side view.

12c

Twist the hip and stamp down with the right foot. Block to stomach level with the right elbow.

13

Right-hand back-fist strike, uraken-uchi, ensuring that the arm moves in the vertical plane. Snap the fist back to the hip following the same path.

13

Side view.

14a

Lift the left knee.

14b

Twist the hip and stamp down with the left foot. Block to stomach level with the left elbow.

15

Left-hand back-fist strike, uraken-uchi, ensuring that the arm moves in the vertical plane. Snap the fist back to the hip following the same path.

16a

Lift the right knee.

16b

Twist the hip and stamp down with the right foot. Block to stomach level with the right elbow.

17

Right back-fist strike, uraken-uchi, ensuring that the arm moves in the vertical plane. Snap the fist back to the hip following the same path.

18a

Block to right-side vertical knife-hand.

18a

Side view.

18b

Immediately step forward with the left foot and execute stepping punch.

18b

Side view.

19a

Bring the right foot up alongside the left foot.

19b

Move the left foot around and turn 180 degrees anticlockwise. Bring the left fist to the hip and the right fist over the left shoulder.

20

Slide to the right and move the right foot and then the left foot, yori ashi. Bring the right fist to the hip and the left fist over the right shoulder. Kiai.

Finish by moving the left foot across into ready stance and bowing.

KATA APPLICATION

This is a simple application of moves 14 and 15 in Heian Sandan that will help in developing these techniques. You will notice that if the back-fist strike does not follow the correct path, the opponent's arm will obstruct it.

1

The attacker prepares to attack with a stepping punch.

2

As the attacker punches, the defender steps back and blocks using the left elbow.

3

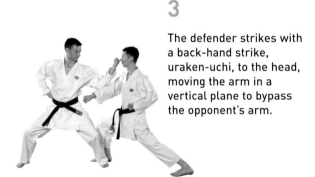

The defender strikes with a back-hand strike, uraken-uchi, to the head, moving the arm in a vertical plane to bypass the opponent's arm.

Basic One-Step Sparring

Kihon Ippon Kumite

Basic one-step sparring, kihon ippon kumite, is quite similar to gohon kumite, except that there is only one attack and counterattack before the exchange is stopped. The defender must respond with a counterattacking technique after every block. This may be a technique of the defender's own choice, but the simplest (and hence most reliable) counterattack is the reverse punch.

In one-step sparring, the attacker should perform the head-level attack followed by the stomach-level attack using right-hand side attacks as illustrated in Chapter 3, with the defender using the left hand to block. The attacker then continues to do the same attacks using left-hand side attacks with the defender using the right hand to block.

CHAPTER **SEVEN** green to purple belt

The green belt syllabus introduces the roundhouse kick, mawashi-geri, that has become so popular in freestyle sparring. A green belt is expected to be able to use kicks in sparring, and this, along with the athletically demanding kata Heian Yondan, means that the green belt level requires good flexibility.

Syllabus Summary

Green belt gradings follow the following format:

GREEN BELT GRADING SYLLABUS	
Basics	
Triple punch	Sanbon tsuki
Rising block, reverse punch, downward block	Age-uke, gyaku-zuki, gedan barai
Outside block, elbow strike, back-fist strike	Soto-uke, empi-uchi, uraken-uchi
Inside block, jabbing punch, reverse punch	Uchi-uke, kizami-zuki, gyaku-zuki
Knife-hand block, jabbing front kick, spear-hand strike	Shuto-uke, kizami mae-geri, nukite
Consecutive front kicks	Mae ren-geri
Side thrusting kick	Yoko kekomi
Side rising kick	Yoko keage
Roundhouse kick	Mawashi-geri
Kata	
Heian Yondan	
Kumite	
One-step sparring	Ippon kumite
Head-level stepping punch	Jodan oi-zuki
Stomach-level stepping punch	Chudan oi-zuki
Front kick	Mae-geri
Side thrusting kick	Yoko kekomi

Basic Form

OUTSIDE BLOCK, ELBOW STRIKE, BACK-FIST STRIKE
Soto-uke, Empi-uchi, Uraken-uchi

Make sure that the block is performed to completion. A common mistake is to rush from the block to the next move, resulting in a weak blocking technique. Conversely, try to use the momentum of the body while executing the elbow strike to fire off the back-fist strike. The correct timing for the combination should be block, pause, elbow strike, back-fist strike. The back-fist strike should be done with a whipping action.

1

Start in front stance, zenkutsu-dachi.

2

Step forward and block to stomach level with outside block, soto-uke.

3

On the spot, shift your weight into side stance, kiba-dachi, and strike with the elbow, empi-uchi.

4

Strike with back-fist, uraken-uchi.

5

Snap back the fist.

INSIDE BLOCK, JABBING PUNCH, REVERSE PUNCH

Uchi-uke, Kizami-zuki, Gyaku-zuki

As with the previous technique, make sure that the block is performed to completion. A common mistake is to rush from the block to the next move, resulting in a weak blocking technique. When punching with the leading hand, try to use as much of the body as possible to generate power and not just the arm. A good timing to use is block, pause, punch, punch.

1

Start in front stance, zenkutsu-dachi.

2

Step forward and block to stomach level with an inside block, uchi-uke.

3

Without stepping, punch using the leading hand, kizami-zuki.

4

Without stepping, reverse punch, gyaku-zuki.

KNIFE-HAND BLOCK, JABBING FRONT KICK, SPEAR-HAND STRIKE

Shuto-uke, Kizami Mae-geri, Nukite-uchi

Make sure that the block is performed to completion and in the correct stance. When kicking, try not to bring your body weight back more than necessary. If you can leave your weight forward, you will be able to make a fast transition and transfer power to the spear-hand strike.

1

Start in back stance, kokutsu-dachi.

2

Step forward into back stance and block with a stomach-level knife-hand block, shuto-uke.

3

Without stepping, lift the front leg and execute front kick, mae-geri.

4

Without stepping, shift your body weight forward and strike to stomach level with spear-hand strike, nukite-uchi.

ROUNDHOUSE KICK

Mawashi-geri

The basic roundhouse kick should be done with as big a rotation as possible. Make sure that, when rotating, you pivot your supporting foot. Failure to do this can result in injuring your ankle. The striking area is the ball of the foot, but for sparring it is possible to use the top of the foot instead.

1

Start in freestyle front stance.

2

Lift the rear leg.

3

Swing the hips around so that you rotate on the supporting leg and execute roundhouse kick, mawashi-geri.

4

Snap back the kicking foot.

5

Step forward into front stance.

CROSS BLOCK
Juji-uke

1

Start in front stance,
zenkutsu-dachi.

2

Raise both arms to the right
shoulder with the right fist
on top.

3

Step forward into front
stance and block down, as if
blocking left-hand gedan
barai and punching the right
hand.

KNIFE-HAND STRIKE

Shuto-uchi

The strike should be with the fleshy base of the hand with the palm up. It should be delivered in a tight circular path.

1

Start in front stance, zenkutsu-dachi.

2

Prepare to strike with the left hand by pulling it back. Reach forward with the right hand.

3

Strike to head level with knife-hand strike, shuto-uchi.

93

WEDGE BLOCK
Kakiwake-uke

1

Start in ready stance.

2

Bring both fists to the hips.

3

Slowly start to step forward while crossing the arms in front of the body, palm side facing in.

4

Step out into back stance and slowly open the arms and rotate so that the palm side faces out.

4

Kakiwake-uke, close-up view.

Heian Yondan

This is the fourth kata in the Heian series. Heian Yondan is the most athletically challenging of the Heian kata and contains no less than five kicks, which require leg flexibility to both the front and the side. This kata also makes extensive use of both slow and fast techniques. Demonstrating a good contrast between these techniques is critical to performing this kata well.

KATA SEQUENCE

Bow. Announce the kata 'Heian Yondan' and step into ready stance.

1

Step to the left into back stance, kokutsu-dachi. With open hands, slowly raise your arms, blocking upper-level inside block with the left arm and rising block with the right.

2

Pivot into back stance facing the other way. With open hands, slowly raise your arms, blocking upper-level inside block with the right arm and rising block with the left.

3

Step to the left and block with a lower-level cross-block, gedan juji-uke.

4

Step forward into back stance, kokutsu-dachi, and block right-side double-handed block, morote-uke.

5

Pull the left leg up to the right knee, place both fists on the right hip and look to the left.

6

Kick to the left side with side rising kick, yoko keage, and simultaneously strike with left back-fist strike, uraken-uchi.

7

Snap the foot back (but leave the left hand) and step down into front stance. Simultaneously, open the left hand and strike into it with the right elbow, empi-uchi.

8

Shift the left foot halfway toward the right and then lift the right foot onto the knee. Place both fists on the left hip and look to the right.

9

Kick to the right side with a side rising kick, yoko keage, and simultaneously strike with right back-fist strike, uraken-uchi.

10

Snap the foot back (but leave the right hand out) and step down into front stance. Simultaneously, open the right hand and strike into it with the left elbow, empi-uchi.

11a

Using open hands, block to lower level with the left and upper level with the right.

11b

Using open hands, block to upper level with the left and strike knife-hand to head level, jodan shuto-uchi.

12a

Kick stomach-level front kick, mae-geri chudan, with the right foot.

12a

Side view.

12b

Snap the leg back and simultaneously reach forward with the left hand in a pressing block while lifting the right fist above the head.

12c

Both hands keep moving in a circular motion so that the left fist comes to the left hip and the right hand performs a back-fist strike, uraken-uchi, while stepping forwards into crossed leg stance, kosa-dachi. Kiai.

12c

Side view.

13

In a slow and controlled movement, pivot 135 degrees anticlockwise and step out with the left leg into back stance. Simultaneously, cross the arms, palms toward you, with the left arm on the outside. Open the arms, rotating the wrists out into wedge block, kakiwake-uke.

14

Front kick to head level, jodan mae-geri, with the right leg.

15

Step down into front stance and immediately punch to stomach level, chudan oi-zuki, with the right fist.

16

Punch to stomach level, chudan gyaku-zuki, with the left fist.

17

In a slow and controlled movement, pivot 90 degrees clockwise and step out with the right leg into back stance. Simultaneously, cross the arms, palms toward you, with the right arm on the outside. Open the arms, rotating the wrists out into wedge block, kakiwake-uke.

18

Perform head-level front kick, jodan mae-geri, with the left leg.

19

Step down into front stance and immediately punch to stomach level, chudan oi-zuki, with the left fist.

20

Punch to stomach level, chudan gyaku-zuki, with the right fist.

21

Step 45 degrees to the left into back stance and use double-handed block, morote-uke, with the left side.

22

Step and use double-handed block, morote-uke, with the right side.

23

Step and use double-handed block, morote-uke, with the left side.

24

Move forward into front stance and push the open hands up to head level, palms facing each other as if grabbing someone's head.

24

Side view.

25

Thrust the right knee upward while simultaneously closing the fists and pulling them down to the level of the knee. Kiai.

25

Side view.

26

Pivot anticlockwise to face toward the rear and step into left leg forward back stance with a left knife-hand block, shuto-uke.

27

Step forward with the right foot into back stance with a knife-hand block, shuto-uke.

Finish by moving the right foot back into ready stance and bowing.

KATA APPLICATION

There are many possible applications of moves 11 and 12 in Heian Yondan. These moves consist of simultaneous blocks and strikes followed by a kick and a close-range finishing move. One possible application that will help in developing these techniques is shown here.

1

The attacker punches to stomach level with a right-hand stepping punch. The defender steps into front stance at an angle away from the attack while blocking with the left hand and preparing with the right hand.

2

The attacker follows up with a left punch to head level. The defender deflects the punch with the left hand and strikes to head level with a knife-hand strike, shuto-uchi.

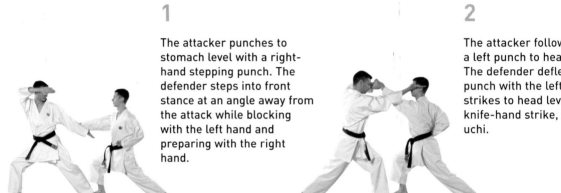

3

The defender kicks to the groin or stomach with front kick, mae-geri.

4

The defender finishes with a downward elbow strike, empi-uchi, to the back of the neck.

As an alternative, the defender finishes with a back-hand strike, uraken-uchi, to the back of the neck.
   Moves 13–16 can be applied to defend against a throttling attack.

1

The attacker uses both hands to grab the throat.

2

The defender steps backward into back stance and uses wedge block, kakiwake-uke, to release pressure on the throat and pull the attacker forward.

3

The defender counterattacks by using a knee strike.

4

The defender continues the counterattack with head-level punches.

Basic One-Step Sparring

FRONT KICK ATTACK

Mae-geri

When defending against a front kick, it is not sufficient to simply step back and block. Trying to parry a powerful front kick using brute force could result in a broken arm. It is therefore important that the defender makes use of lateral motion and steps off the line of the attack using the blocking motion to deflect the kick. This avoids the danger inherent in trying to block a powerful technique, like a front kick, head on. Moreover, by stepping to the inside of the attacker, it opens up greater opportunity for an effective counterattack.

1

Both the attacker and defender start in ready position. The attacker steps back right side with a downward block, gedan barai, and then relaxes the hands to freestyle fighting position and announces the attack: 'Mae-geri!'

2

The attacker performs a right-leg front kick to the body with kiai. The defender steps back and to the right and blocks with a downward block, gedan barai.

3

The defender immediately counterattacks with reverse punch. Kiai. The attacker withdraws, and as he does so, the defender steps up, both finishing in yoi position.

SIDE THRUSTING KICK ATTACK

Yoko Kekomi

Similar to the defense against the front kick, the defender must step off the line of the attack when faced with a side thrusting kick. However, because of the trajectory of the side thrusting kick, this is most successful when stepping to the outside of the attacker.

1

Both the attacker and defender start in the ready position. The attacker steps back right side with a downward block, gedan barai, and then relaxes the hands into freestyle fighting position and announces the attack: 'Yoko kekomi!'

2

The attacker kicks with a right-leg side thrusting kick to the body with a kiai. The defender steps back and to the left and blocks with an outside block, soto-uke.

3

The defender immediately counterattacks with reverse punch with a kiai. The attacker withdraws, and as he does so, the defender steps up, both finishing in ready stance, yoi-dachi.

CHAPTER **EIGHT** purple to purple and white belt

The syllabus between green belt and purple belt changes little, so this is a good grade to try to perfect all the techniques that have gone before. The purple belt kata, Heian Godan, completes the Heian series of kata, and this is an ideal time to ensure that all the Heian kata are known and understood.

Syllabus Summary

Purple belt gradings follow the following format:

PURPLE BELT GRADING SYLLABUS	
Basics	
Triple punch	Sanbon tsuki
Rising block, reverse punch, downward block	Age-uke, gyaku-zuki, gedan barai
Outside block, elbow strike, back-fist strike, reverse punch	Soto-uke, empi-uchi, uraken-uchi, gyaku-zuki
Inside block, jabbing punch, reverse punch	Uchi-uke, kizami-zuki, gyaku-zuki
Knife-hand block, jabbing front kick, spear-hand strike	Shuto-uke, kizami mae-geri, nukite
Consecutive front kicks	Mae ren-geri
Side thrusting kick	Yoko kekomi
Side rising kick	Yoko keage
Roundhouse kick	Mawashi-geri
Kata	
Heian Godan	
Kumite	
One-step sparring	Ippon kumite
Head-level stepping punch	Jodan oi-zuki
Stomach-level stepping punch	Chudan oi-zuki
Front kick	Mae-geri
Side thrusting kick	Yoko kekomi

Basic Form

OUTSIDE BLOCK, ELBOW STRIKE, BACK-FIST STRIKE, REVERSE PUNCH
Soto-uke, Empi-uchi, Uraken-uchi, Gyaku-zuki

Ensure that you use the momentum of the body while executing the elbow strike to fire off the back-fist strike. Snap the fist straight back to the hip while punching with the other hand. Try to keep the arm muscles relaxed so that you get a whipping action on the back-fist strike. Rotating the hips strongly will pull the back-fist back to the hip and simultaneously fire the reverse punch effectively.

1
Start in front stance, zenkutsu-dachi.

2
Step forward and block to stomach level with outside block, soto-uke.

3
On the spot, shift your weight into side stance, kiba-dachi, and strike with the elbow, empi-uchi.

4
Strike with back-fist, uraken-uchi.

5
Shift into front stance and reverse punch, gyaku-zuki.

SWASTIKA BLOCK
Manji-uke

The swastika block, or swastika position, manji gamae, can be described simplistically as a downward sweeping block, gedan barai, with one hand and a simultaneous head-level inside block, jodan uchi-uke, with the other hand. It is, however, a much more complex movement than that suggests and can be used as a throwing action or a grasping/pulling action combined with a strike.

1

Start in front stance, zenkutsu-dachi.

2

Step forward and block open-handed across the face with the left hand, nagashi-uke. Simultaneously, strike to low level with right knife-hand, shuto-uchi.

3

Close the fists and pull with the right hand so that it goes behind your head, with the palm facing toward you. Simultaneously, block down, gedan barai, with the left hand.

The Swastika

The swastika has existed as a religious symbol for thousands of years. For Hindus, it symbolizes well-being and good luck, and it is Sanskrit, the ancient ceremonial language of the Hindu religion, which gives us the word swastika, 'su' meaning good and 'vasti' meaning being. In Buddhist art and literature – as shown here – it is called a manji and represents universal harmony, the balance of opposites. It was not until the 20th century, when the symbol was adopted by Adolf Hitler's Nazi party, that the symbol acquired negative connotations.

CRESCENT KICK, ELBOW STRIKE

Mikazuki-geri, Empi-uchi

Literally translated, mikazuki means crescent moon and describes the crescent-shaped path that the kick follows. When doing the crescent kick, hold back the shoulder and elbow until your foot strikes the target and then strongly rotate the hip forward so that the elbow strike is powerful. To increase the power of the kick and speed of the combination, aim the kick so that its highest point is above the height of the target. This ensures that it is moving downward as it makes contact, which will have the effect of reducing the delay between the kick and the subsequent elbow strike.

1

Start in front stance, zenkutsu-dachi.

2

Reach forward with an open hand.

3

Swing the leg around, keeping the leg relatively straight, and kick into your open hand.

4

Immediately rotate the hip forward and strike with the elbow, empi-uchi, into your open hand, and land in side stance, kiba-dachi.

HOOK PUNCH
Kagi Zuki

The simplest interpretation of the hook punch is a close-range punch that travels around, hitting the target from the side.

1

Start with the right hand on the hip and with the left arm reaching forward.

2

Push the right fist forward as if doing a straight punch to stomach level. Pull back the left hand to the left hip.

3

The right fist curves to the side to complete a hook punch, kagi zuki.

Alternatively, the hook punch action can be used to apply a lock. When applying the lock, the retracting hand is used to pull the opponent's arm and the leading hand is used to apply pressure to the opponent's elbow. You should practice this move as a slow, controlled movement.

1

The attacker starts in front stance with the left leg forward.

2

The attacker steps and punches with the right hand. The defender uses the soto-uke preparation position to block and grab with the right hand.

3

The defender uses the soto-uke motion to attack the elbow.

4

The defender uses a left-hand hook punch action to apply a lock. The stance is shortened by sliding the right foot forward.

Heian Godan

This is the fifth kata in the Heian series of kata. It is characterized primarily by its jumping technique, but it is also important for introducing the manji-uke, which is common in the advanced shotokan kata. Heian Godan also contains sequences that are used in the popular advanced kata, Bassai Dai, which is needed for grading to black belt. Heian Godan thus provides useful preparation for this important kata, but it can also lead to confusion because a lapse in concentration can result in inadvertently crossing over into another kata. For this reason, Heian Godan is popular with grading examiners in brown belt and black belt examinations.

KATA SEQUENCE

Bow. Announce the kata 'Heian Godan' and step into ready stance.

1

Step with the left leg into back stance, kokutsu-dachi. Perform an inside block, uchi-uke, with the left arm.

2

Immediately punch with the right hand, gyaku-zuki, remaining in back stance.

3

Slowly bring the right foot alongside the left foot while simultaneously bringing the left arm into a hook punch position, kagi zuki.

4

Step with the right leg into back stance, kokutsu-dachi. Perform an inside block, uchi-uke, with the left arm.

5

Immediately punch with the left hand, gyaku-zuki, remaining in back stance.

6

Slowly bring the left foot alongside the right foot while simultaneously bringing the right arm into a hook punch position, kagi zuki.

7

Step forward with the right leg into back stance, kokutsu-dachi, while blocking with double-handed block, morote-uke.

8

Step forward into front stance, zenkutsu-dachi, and block with lower-level cross-block, gedan juji-uke.

9a

Pull the hands back to the stomach.

9b

Block to head level with open-handed cross-block, jodan juji-uke.

10

Bring the hands down to the right side of the body just above the belt. They should rotate as they move so they finish with palms together, left on top of right.

11

Without stepping, punch with the left hand.

12

Stepping punch with the right hand. Kiai.

13

Rotate anticlockwise with the left foot as pivot, lift the right knee and stamp down while simultaneously blocking down with the right hand, gedan barai.

13

Side view.

14

Slowly cross arms, right over left. Open the arms slowly and smoothly, blocking with the back of the open hand.

14

Side view.

15

Crescent kick with the right leg into the open hand.

16

Immediately strike into the left palm with the right elbow while stepping down into side stance, kiba-dachi.

16

Side view.

17

Look to the right and use double-handed block while moving the left foot into crossed leg stance, kosa-dachi.

113

18

Upper-cut with the right fist, keeping the left fist on the forearm, and look behind you while moving the left foot into a very short back stance.

18

Side view.

19a

Jump by lifting first the right knee and then the left and rotating 180 degrees. Bring the fists to the hip. Kiai.

19b

Land in crossed leg stance, kosa-dachi, and bring the fists down in a low-level cross block, gedan juji-uke.

20

Step to the right into front stance and use double-handed block, morote-uke.

21

Look over the left shoulder and turn 180 degrees into front stance while blocking across the face with open left hand. Strike to the lower level with right-side knife-hand strike, gedan shuto-uchi.

22

Switch into back stance, kokutsu-dachi, by shifting the weight onto the right foot. Simultaneously, execute swastika block, manji-uke, by pulling the right hand.

22

Side view.

23

Slowly pull the left foot to the right foot and straighten the legs.

24

Step with the right foot forward into front stance while blocking across the face with open right hand and strike to the lower level with left-side knife-hand strike, gedan shuto-uchi.

25

Shift the weight back into back stance, kokutsu-dachi, with swastika block, manji-uke, by pulling the left hand.

Finish by moving the right foot back into ready stance and bowing.

KATA APPLICATION

This is a simple application of moves 14, 15 and 16 in Heian Godan. It starts with a technique that is usually referred to as a block, but it is performed slowly in the kata, suggesting a locking or breaking technique.

1

The attacker grabs the collar from behind.

2

The defender turns, drags his fingers across the attacker's face and tries to catch the attacker's arm under the armpit.

3

The defender grabs the attacker and strikes with crescent kick to the back of the knee.

4

The defender strikes to the attacker's head using elbow strike.

Below is a simple application of moves 21 and 22 in Heian Godan. The swastika block is often described as a simultaneous downward block and head-level inside block. There is, however, no credible explanation for why someone would do two blocks at the same time, especially in opposite directions. More realistically, one hand is doing a pulling action while the other strikes or unbalances the opponent.

1

The attacker starts with the right leg forward and the defender starts in natural stance.

2

The attacker punches to head level with a left-hand stepping punch. The defender steps into front stance and blocks across the face with the left hand while striking down to the opponent's leg with the right hand.

3

The defender strikes down with the left fist while simultaneously pulling with the right hand, thus unbalancing the attacker.

JUMPING IN HEIAN GODAN

This is a breakdown of how to do the jump, move 19, from Heian Godan. The jump should be done smoothly and quickly. The objective is to jump upward rather than across, although there is still some lateral movement. This upward motion should be achieved more by lifting and tucking the legs than by raising the center of mass.

1

Rotate by lifting the right knee to the chest. Bring the fists to the hips.

2

Lift the left leg and tuck the left ankle on top of the right ankle.

3

Land in crossed leg stance with the left foot behind the right foot and block down with cross block, juji-uke. Make sure your back is straight.

CHAPTER **NINE** purple and white to brown belt

Purple and white belt represents the last of the intermediate grades and is the gateway to the advanced grades of brown belt and beyond. Beyond this grade, the syllabus is very different. It's therefore important for purple and white belt students to perfect their set of techniques so that they are ready to move on to new things. Students at this grade should make a special effort to perfect the focus (kime) of their techniques. This is a very important aspect of karate training and one that is especially crucial for the purple and white belt kata, Tekki Shodan.

Syllabus Summary
Purple and white belt gradings follow the following format:

PURPLE AND WHITE BELT GRADING SYLLABUS	
Basics	
Triple punch	Sanbon tsuki
Rising block, reverse punch, downward block	Age-uke, gyaku-zuki, gedan barai
Outside block, elbow strike, back-fist strike, reverse punch, downward block	Soto-uke, empi-uchi, uraken-uchi, gyaku-zuki, gedan barai
Inside block, jabbing punch, reverse punch, downward block	Uchi-uke, kizami-zuki, gyaku-zuki, gedan barai
Knife-hand block, jabbing front kick, spear-hand strike	Shuto-uke, kizami mae-geri, nukite
Consecutive front kicks	Mae ren-geri
Side thrusting kick	Yoko kekomi
Side rising kick	Yoko keage
Roundhouse kick	Mawashi-geri
Back kick	Ushiro-geri
Kata	
Tekki Shodan	
Kumite	
One-step sparring	Ippon kumite

Head-level stepping punch	Jodan Oi-zuki
Stomach-level stepping punch	Chudan Oi-zuki
Front kick	Mae-geri
Side thrusting kick	Yoko kekomi
Roundhouse kick	Mawashi-geri

Basic Form

OUTSIDE BLOCK, ELBOW STRIKE, BACK-FIST STRIKE, REVERSE PUNCH, DOWNWARD BLOCK

Soto-uke, Empi-uchi, Uraken-uchi, Gyaku-zuki, Gedan Barai

Ensure that no techniques are lost in this long combination. The first block must be strong with good focus (kime). Use natural flow to make the best use of your momentum for the next three moves while keeping each move large and distinct. Ensure that the last move is as strong as all the others. A good timing is block, pause, strike, strike, punch, pause, block.

1

Start in front stance, zenkutsu-dachi.

2

Step forward and block to stomach level with outside block, soto-uke.

3

On the spot, shift your weight into side stance, kiba-dachi, and strike with the elbow, empi-uchi.

4

Strike with back-fist, uraken-uchi.

5

Shift into front stance and reverse punch, gyaku-zuki.

6

Downward block, gedan barai.

INSIDE BLOCK, JABBING PUNCH, REVERSE PUNCH, DOWNWARD BLOCK
Uchi-uke, Kizame-zuki, Gyaku-zuki, Gedan Barai

1

Start in front stance, zenkutsu-dachi.

2

Step forward and block to stomach level with outside block, uchi-uke.

3

Without stepping, punch using the leading hand, kizame-zuki.

4

Without stepping, reverse punch, gyaku-zuki.

5

Downward block, gedan barai.

RETURNING WAVE KICK

Nami Gaeshi-geri

The returning wave kick is a short lifting kick that moves in a short arc. It can be used as a tripping attack and is the basis for leg sweeps, ashi barai, which are common in freestyle sparring. This kick can be practiced in side stance using the hand as a target.

1

Start in side stance, kiba-dachi.

2

Without shifting your weight, lift the foot and strike your hands using the bottom of the foot.

Common Mistakes

Don't kick the opposite leg.

Don't shift your balance on to the grounded leg. Instead, kick faster and keep your body weight low.

BACK KICK

Ushiro-geri

It is important to kick along your centerline. In this regard, it is similar to the front kick. Ensure that the recoil is as strong as the kick itself. This will help drive you forward into your next move (which in this case is just to return to fighting posture).

1

Start in freestyle stance. Keep the weight on the balls of the feet. Use a narrow stance.

2

Rotate around the left hip. The hips should move forward.

3

Coil the leg, ready to kick.

4

Kick.

5

Recoil the leg along the line of the kick.

6

Step down.

Common Mistakes

Incorrect path

The back kick is done all on one line. A common mistake is to let the leg swing out away from that line. To correct this, keep the knees together when starting the kick.

Incorrect form: the leg swings out

Correct form: the leg goes back in a straight line

Incorrect withdrawal

After kicking, a common mistake is to fail to pull the knee back. To correct this, focus on pulling the knee back along the path that the kick followed.

Incorrect form: the leg 'hooks' back after the kick

Correct form: the leg pulled back by the retracting knee

Tekki Shodan

This is the first kata in the Tekki series of kata. The kanji for Tekki is made up of two characters, one meaning iron and the other meaning horse. It was originally called Naihanchi (and before that Naifanchi, using the Chinese pronunciation) and was introduced to Okinawa by Sokon Matsumura. Some stories say that he learned the kata in China, but this is by no means certain, and he may well have developed it himself. It was obviously a very important kata to the karate masters in Shuri – Itosu is said to have made Gichin Funakoshi practice Naihanchi for three years. This seems strange considering that Shuri-te, which shotokan is based on, is concerned primarily with linear strikes, and these signature moves are absent from Tekki Shodan.

When performing the kata, use the upper body to make the moves as big and as strong as possible while still maintaining a good side stance (kiba-dachi). It is essential that you use strong, focused techniques to emphasize the strength of the arm movements.

KATA SEQUENCE
Bow. Announce the kata 'Tekki Shodan.'

Put the feet together. Place the left hand over the right hand with the fingertips touching.

1

Bend the knees and step with the left foot in front of the right foot.

2a

Lift the right knee.

2b

Stamp down with the right foot landing in side stance, kiba-dachi, and simultaneously block with the back of the right hand to the right.

3

Pull back the right hand and elbow strike, empi-uchi, into it with the left elbow.

4

Pull both hands to the right hip, left on top of right, and look to the left.

5

Downward block, gedan barai, to the left with the left arm.

6

Hook punch, kagi zuki, to the left with the right hand.

7

Step across to the left with the right foot in front of the left foot.

8a

Lift the left knee.

8b

Stamp down with the left foot into kiba-dachi. At the same time, bring the left fist to the right shoulder and execute inside block, uchi-uke.

9a

Cross the arms, with the left arm on the outside. Straighten the right arm and bring the left hand up on the left side of the head in upper-level sweeping block, jodan nagashi-uke.

9b

Back-fist strike with the left hand and simultaneously bend the right arm, bringing the right hand under the left elbow.

10

Look to the left.

11a

Returning wave kick, nami gaeshi-geri, with the left foot.

11b

Swing the arms to the left, rotating the left palm away from you.

12

Look to the right.

13a

Returning wave kick, nami gaeshi-geri, with the right foot.

13b

Swing the arms to the right, rotating the left palm toward you.

14a

Bring hands to the right hip, the left on top of the right, and look to the left.

14b

Left-hand hammer-fist strike and right-hand hook punch, kagi zuki, to the left. Kiai.

15

Smoothly cross and open the arms with a continuous movement, blocking to the left with the back of the left hand.

16

Pull back the left hand and elbow strike, empi-uchi, into it with the right elbow.

17

Pull both hands to the left hip, right on top of left, and look to the right.

18

Downward block, gedan barai, to the right with the right arm.

19

Hook punch, kagi zuki, to the right with the left hand.

20

Step across to the right with the left foot in front of the right foot.

21a

Lift the right knee.

21b

Stamp down with the right foot into kiba-dachi. At the same time, bring the left fist to the right shoulder and execute inside block, uchi-uke.

22a

Cross the arms, with the right arm on the outside. Straighten the left arm and bring the right hand up on the right side of the head in upper-level sweeping block, jodan nagashi-uke.

22b

Strike back-fist with the right hand and simultaneously bend the left arm, bringing the left hand under the right elbow.

23

Look to the right.

24a

Returning wave kick, nami gaeshi-geri, with the right foot.

24b

Swing the arms to the right, rotating the right palm away from you.

25

Look to the left.

26a

Returning wave kick, nami gaeshi-geri, with the left foot.

26b

Swing the arms to the left, rotating the right palm toward you.

27a

Bring the hands to the left hip, the right on top of the left. Look to the right.

27b

Right-hand hammer-fist strike and left-hand hook punch, kagi zuki, to the right. Kiai.

Finish by moving the right foot to the left and the left hand over the right hand with the fingertips touching. Bow.

KATA APPLICATION

This is a simple application of moves 23 to 26 in Tekki Shodan. Note that both kicks attack the same knee.

1

The attacker grabs with both hands.

2

The defender grabs the attacker and uses a right-foot returning wave kick to attack the right knee.

3

The defender pulls the attacker to the right using both hands.

4

The defender uses a left-foot returning wave kick to attack the right knee.

5

The defender pulls the attacker to the left using both hands.

Below is a simple application of moves 2 to 6 in Tekki Shodan. Please note that this is a very dangerous technique. If it is practiced with a partner, it should be performed only at slow speed for reasons of safety.

1

The attacker grabs with the right hand.

2

The defender uses the right arm to lock the grabbing arm and lifts his right knee, swinging it down behind the attacker's right knee.

3

The defender strikes the head or ribs with an elbow strike.

4

The defender grabs the head and pulls it into the hip.

5

The defender rotates the neck in a devastating neck break.

135

Basic One-Step Sparring

ROUNDHOUSE KICK ATTACK
Mawashi-geri

1

Both the attacker and the defender start in the ready position. The attacker steps back with the right foot with a downward block, gedan barai, and then relaxes the hands to freestyle fighting position and announces the attack: 'Mawashi-geri!'

2

The attacker performs a right-leg roundhouse kick to the head with kiai. The defender steps back and to the right and blocks with an inside block, uchi-uke.

3

The defender immediately counterattacks using a reverse punch with kiai. The attacker withdraws, and as he does so, the defender steps up, both finishing in ready stance, yoi-dachi.

CHAPTER **TEN** brown to black belt

Upon reaching brown belt, you will now be considered a senior grade in your club, and even though you have a lot to learn for black belt, lower grades will already be looking up to you to set standards and offer technical guidance.

At this level, there is a step change in the syllabus format. The basics will have more focus on kicking combinations, and on top of these new combinations you will still be expected to remember all the combinations you learned for previous gradings. You will also be expected to be able to pick up new combinations quickly and to perform them fluidly.

The kata that you have to learn, Bassai Dai, is double the length of the previous kata and requires more study to learn and greater stamina to perform. There is also now a greater emphasis on sparring. From this point, you have about one year to train for black belt.

Syllabus Summary

Brown belt gradings (that is to say, grading to brown belt with a white stripe and grading to brown belt with two white stripes) follow the following format:

BROWN BELT GRADING SYLLABUS	
Basics	
Triple punch	Kizami-zuki, oi-zuki, gyaku-zuki
Front kick combination	Mae-geri, oi-zuki, gyaku-zuki
Side thrusting kick combination	Yoko kekomi, uraken-uchi, gyaku-zuki
Roundhouse kick combination	Mawashi-geri, uraken-uchi, gyaku-zuki
Back kick combination	Ushiro-geri, uraken-uchi, gyaku-zuki
Kata	
Bassai Dai	
Kumite	
One-step free sparring	Jiyu ippon kumite
Head-level stepping punch	Jodan oi-zuki
Stomach-level stepping punch	Chudan oi-zuki

Front kick	Mae-geri
Side thrusting kick	Yoko kekomi
Roundhouse kick	Mawashi-geri
Back kick	Ushiro-geri

In addition, when grading to black belt, you will be expected to demonstrate the following:

BLACK BELT GRADING SYLLABUS

Basics

Four-kick combination	Mae-geri, yoko kekomi, mawashi-geri, ushiro-geri, uraken-uchi, gyaku-zuki
Standing kicks	Mae-geri, yoko kekomi, ushiro-geri
Black belt combination	

Kata

Choose one from

Bassai Dai, Kanku Dai, Jion, Empi, Hangetsu

Kumite

Free sparring	Jiyu-kumite

Fundamentals

When performing the brown belt basic form, remember the basic form from previous grades because it still applies. Do not abandon what you have learned before: really the only difference at this level is that you start and finish in free-fighting stance. This means that you should still endeavor to use low, long stances during the sequences and use big, fully completed techniques.

FIGHTING STANCE

Kamae

The fighting stance is not a formally defined stance, but consider the following:

- Point the front foot in the direction that you are going.

- Put your weight over the front foot and on the ball of the foot.

- Have your body turned to the side but the head turned to the front.

- Hold your hands up in a guard with the fists pointing at your target.

The fighting stance, kamae

Basic Form

TRIPLE PUNCH

The triple punch combination should be a continuous stream of punches. Try to keep pauses between the attacks to a minimum by pushing your weight forward over the front foot when doing the first punch. This has the effect of not only increasing the range and power of this punch, but also of allowing the second punch, the stepping punch, to proceed more rapidly.

Each time you punch, you must pull back the opposite fist to your hip. This is important because it encourages a stronger, more committed punch and also allows a bigger, and therefore more powerful, motion on the next punch.

It is not just during the punching combination that you have to worry about pulling back the reverse hand. The same advice also applies to the kicking combinations. It is a common mistake throughout all the brown belt combinations to focus on the punching hand and leave the other hand 'floating.'

1

Start in fighting stance with the left leg forward.

2

On the spot, punch with the leading hand, kizame-zuki.

3

Stepping punch, oi-zuki.

4

Reverse punch, gyaku-zuki. Lock-out the technique briefly before returning to fighting stance, kamae.

FRONT KICK COMBINATION

When kicking with a front kick, you should not change your hand position. Only as you finish the kick and your foot touches the ground should you allow the arms to move as you unleash the punch. As with the triple punch combination, it is important to pull back the reverse hand when punching.

1

Start in fighting stance with the left leg forward.

2

Front kick, mae-geri, with the right foot.

3

As you land, punch with the right hand, oi-zuki.

4

Reverse punch with the left hand. Lock-out the technique briefly before returning to fighting stance, kamae.

SIDE THRUSTING KICK COMBINATION

When you kick with the side thrusting kick, ensure that you commit the hip. Remember to lock the kick in position because this is a thrust kick. Pull back the leg strongly: this will actually help you move forward faster for the next move.

Each time you kick, check that you are pushing the hip as much as you can. Failing to use the hip correctly will make the kick look weak and uncommitted.

1

Start in fighting stance with the left leg forward.

2

Side thrusting kick, yoko kekomi, with the right foot.

3

Back-fist strike, uraken-uchi, with the right hand.

4

Reverse punch with the left hand. Lock-out the technique briefly before returning to fighting stance, kamae.

ROUNDHOUSE KICK COMBINATION

There are two ways of doing the roundhouse kick. The first is to try to swing the leg through the target. This way maximizes the power of the kick at the expense of range and is appropriate when practicing by kicking a bag or strike shield. The second way is to focus on range by pushing your hips forward toward the target, and rather than swinging through the target, instead snap the foot back. You should use this method when practicing kicking in the air or with a partner.

1

Start in fighting stance with the left leg forward.

2

Roundhouse kick, mawashi-geri, with the right foot.

3

Back-fist strike, uraken-uchi, with the right hand.

4

Reverse punch with the left hand. Lock-out the technique briefly before returning to fighting stance, kamae.

BACK KICK COMBINATION

Sometimes you will be asked to do this combination without step 3, the back-fist strike, and instead proceed straight to the reverse punch. You should be able to demonstrate this combination with and without the back-fist strike.

1

Start in fighting stance with the left leg forward.

2

Back kick, ushiro-geri, with the right foot.

3

Back-fist strike, uraken-uchi, with the right hand.

4

Reverse punch with the left hand. Lock-out the technique briefly before returning to fighting stance, kamae.

FOUR-KICK COMBINATION

1 Start in fighting stance with the left leg forward.

2 Front kick, mae-geri, with the right foot.

3 Side thrusting kick, yoko kekomi, with the left foot.

4 Roundhouse kick, mawashi-geri, with the right foot.

5 Back kick, ushiro-geri, with the left foot.

6 Back-fist strike, uraken-uchi, with the left hand.

7 Reverse punch, gyaku-zuki, with the right hand. Lock-out the technique briefly before returning to fighting stance, kamae.

147

STANDING KICKS

Make sure that you regain balance between kicks. Trying to kick while off balance will result in a weak kick.

1

Start in fighting stance with the left leg forward.

2

Front kick, mae-geri, with the right foot.

3

Without stepping down, do a side thrusting kick, yoko kekomi, with the same foot.

4

Without stepping down, back kick, ushiro-geri, with the same foot.

5

Return to fighting stance.

BLACK BELT COMBINATION

At black belt level, you will be expected to intermix techniques to form long combinations. The following combination is commonly asked for at black belt gradings.

1

Start in fighting stance with the left leg forward.

2

Front kick, mae-geri, with the right foot.

3

Punch with the right hand.

4

Reverse punch with the left hand.

5

Step back and block with left-side downward block, gedan barai.

6

Reverse punch with the right hand.

7

Roundhouse kick, mawashi-geri, with the right foot.

8

Back-fist strike, uraken-uchi, with the right hand.

9

Stepping punch, oi-zuki, with the left hand.

10

Immediately snap the fist back and return to fighting stance, kamae.

Bassai Dai

Bassai, originally called Passai in Okinawa, is most often translated as 'storm a fortress.' However, it is more likely that it means 'extract from a fortress.' Nobody really knows for sure what the name means, but I like to think that, in view of Matsumura and Itosu's roles as bodyguards to the king, they would have had rescuing the king from Shuri Castle in mind when they practiced this kata.

There are many versions of Bassai (Masatoshi Nakayama estimated that there were hundreds), about 11 of which are still practiced today. In creating shotokan karate, Master Gichin Funakoshi selected the version he considered the most effective as one of the 15 core shotokan kata. This version of Bassai became referred to as Bassai Dai, with another well-known variation termed Bassai Sho. Here Dai means 'big' or 'major' and Sho means 'small' or 'minor' the implication being that the Dai version should be practiced first (being one of Funakoshi's 15 core kata), whereas the Sho version is considered only as an auxiliary.

Bassai Dai was demonstrated for the first time in Japan by Gichin Funakoshi in 1922. Today it is one of the most popular kata practiced throughout the various branches of karate and is often used as the main test kata for shodan (black belt) grading. It is twice the length of the kata that precede it (Heian series and Tekki Shodan), and it requires good physical fitness to perform from start to finish at full power.

KATA SEQUENCE
Bow. Announce the kata 'Bassai Dai.'

Put the feet together and clasp the right fist in the left hand.

1a

Swing the arms back to the left side and shift the weight forward ready to move. (Funakoshi added a knee-lift here, but this was later removed by Nakayama. Today both forms are followed.)

1b

Strike forward with the back of the right fist. The left hand is placed on the right forearm. Simultaneously, step forward with the right foot and tuck the left foot behind the right.

2

Turn using the left foot into front stance. Inside block, uchi-uke, with the left hand.

3

Without stepping, block right-hand inside block, uchi-uke.

4

Turn and block left-hand outside block, soto-uke.

5

Without stepping, block right-hand inside block, uchi-uke.

6a

Bring the right foot back alongside the left and do a right-hand low-level sweeping block.

6b

Continue the sweeping movement so that the hand moves all the way up to head height.

6c

Step into front stance with the right foot. Outside block, soto-uke, with the right hand.

7

Without stepping, block left-hand inside block, uchi-uke.

8

Move the left foot into a shoulder-width stance and bring both fists to the right hip.

9

Using slow, controlled movement, make a vertical knife-hand block, tate shuto-uke, with the left hand.

10

Without stepping, punch using the right hand.

153

11

Pull the right hand to the shoulder. Inside block, uchi-uke, pivoting on the spot.

12

Straighten the hips and punch with the left hand.

13

Pull the left hand to the shoulder. Inside block, uchi-uke, pivoting on the spot.

14

Step forward with the right leg into back stance with knife-hand block, shuto-uke.

15

Step forward with the left leg into back stance with knife-hand block, shuto-uke.

16

Step forward with the right leg into back stance with knife-hand block, shuto-uke.

17

Immediately step back with the right leg into back stance with knife-hand block, shuto-uke.

18

Shift into front stance while the right hand reaches up and catches. Pull the right hand back using grasping block, Tsukami-uke.

19

Low-level side thrusting kick with the right foot while the fists pull up to the ribcage. Kiai.

20

Step into back stance with knife-hand block, shuto-uke.

21

Step forward with the right leg into back stance with knife-hand block, shuto-uke.

22

Slowly move the right foot back to meet the left and raise both arms into a double rising block position, morote-age-uke.

23a

Abruptly pull the arms apart and shift the weight forward.

23b

Immediately step forward with the right foot into front stance and strike to stomach level with a double hammer-fist strike, tetsui-uchi.

23b

Side view.

24

Immediately slide forward and punch with the right fist, oi-zuki.

25

Turn and strike right knife-hand, shuto-uchi, while blocking open-handed across the face with the left hand.

26

Slowly draw the left foot back to the right while pulling the right fist up behind the head and blocking down slowly with the left, gedan barai.

26

Side view.

27

Lift the right knee and stamp down into side stance, kiba-dachi, and simultaneously downward block with the left hand, gedan barai.

28

Slowly cross and uncross the arms, blocking open-handed to the left with the back of the hand.

28

Side view.

29

Crescent kick, mikazuki-geri, with the right foot into the left hand.

30

Elbow strike, empi-uchi, with the right elbow into the left hand.

30

Side view.

31

Punch down with the right hand, bringing the left fist up to the inside of the right elbow.

31

Side view.

32

Punch down with the left hand, bringing the right fist up to the inside of the left elbow.

33

Punch down with the right hand, bringing the left fist up to the inside of the right elbow.

34

Bring both fists to the left hip and look to the right. Step out with the right foot into a narrow front stance and attack with both fists: right fist to stomach level, left fist over the head. This is known as a mountain punch, yama-zuki.

34

Side view.

35

Slowly draw the right foot back to meet the left and bring both fists to the right hip.

157

36

Lift the left knee and step forward with mountain punch, yama-zuki: left fist to stomach level, right fist over the head.

37

Slowly draw the left foot back to meet the right and bring both fists to the left hip.

38

Lift the right knee and step forward with mountain punch, yama-zuki: right fist to stomach level, left fist over the head.

39a

Extend the right arm up and look over the left shoulder, pulling the left hand to the hip.

39b

Turn by moving the left foot anticlockwise and swing the right arm across the body in a scooping block.

40a

Extend the left arm.

40b

Pivot and swing the left arm across the body in a scooping block. Finish with a closed fist, palm side up.

41

Move the left foot to your center point. Then step forward with the right foot through 45 degrees into back stance with knife-hand block, shuto-uke.

42

Look over the left shoulder and then slowly move the right foot so that you rotate 90 degrees clockwise.

43

Step with the right foot to your center point. Then step forward with the left foot into back stance with knife-hand block, shuto-uke. Kiai.

Finish by slowly drawing the left foot back to the right and clasping the right fist in the left hand. Bow.

KATA DETAILS
Grasping Block, Side Thrusting Kick
Tsukami-uke, Yoko Kekomi

1

Start in back stance, kokutsu-dachi.

2

The right hand moves up and 'picks up' the left hand.

3

The right hand turns over into grasping block, Tsukami-uke, and pulls down.

4

The right knee pulls up between the arms.

5

Kick down to lower level with side thrusting kick, yoko kekomi.

Mountain Punch

Yama-zuki

Moves 34, 36 and 38 from Bassai Dai are referred to as mountain punches. They are so named because the shape of the body while doing the technique looks a bit like the Japanese kanji symbol for mountain, yama, rotated on its side.

The kanji for mountain, yama

The mountain punch, yama-zuki

Correct Form

1 The upper arm is slightly inclined downward.

2 The punching hands are in line, as if against a wall.

3 The lower arm is slightly inclined upward.

4 Long narrow stance.

161

KATA APPLICATION

The first application is of moves 17 to 19 in Bassai Dai.

1

The attacker punches with
the right hand. The defender
uses a knife-hand block to
deflect the attack.

2

The defender uses grasping
block, tsukami-uke, to apply
a wrist lock.

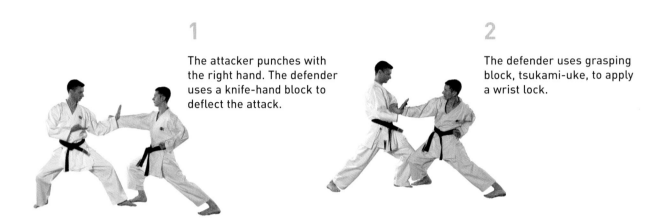

3

The defender lifts the knee
and uses side thrusting kick
to attack the knee.

The next application is of moves 28 to 31 in Bassai Dai.

1

The attacker grabs with the left hand from the left side.

2

The defender uses the left hand to grab the arm while trapping it under the armpit.

3

The defender swings the right leg over the trapped arm, bringing the attacker down.

4

The defender uses an elbow strike to attack the head.

5

The defender grabs the hair with the left hand and twists the head in a devastating neck break by pushing on the chin with the right fist and pulling with the left.

6

This action is repeated so the head is twisted back and forth.

One-step Free Sparring

Jiyu Ippon Kumite

At the advanced level, the formal stances in sparring are dispensed with, so one-step free sparring is performed from a free-fighting position. You should still continue the practice of bowing to your partner before and after sparring, and you must also announce each attack. You are free to move around before attacking but do not get carried away and move without a purpose. The objective of your movement should be to improve your attack. When defending, you must also be light on your feet and should move and block as necessary to avoid being hit while still being able to make a swift and effective counterattack.

HEAD-LEVEL STEPPING PUNCH

Jodan Oi-zuki

1

Both opponents start in free-fighting stance, and the attacker announces 'Jodan!'

2

The attacker steps and punches to the head, oi-zuki. The defender slides back and blocks with rising block, age-uke.

3

The defender punches with the reverse hand, gyaku-zuki.

STOMACH-LEVEL STEPPING PUNCH
Chudan Oi-zuki

1

Both opponents start in free-fighting stance, and the attacker announces 'Chudan!'

2

The attacker steps and punches to the stomach, oi-zuki. The defender slides back and blocks with outside block, soto-uke.

3

The defender punches with the reverse hand, gyaku-zuki.

FRONT KICK
Mae-geri

A common mistake is to kick and then land too near to punch comfortably. Pushing the hips forward on the kick allows you to start a bit further away. As a result, you will be just the right distance away to do the punches.

1

Both opponents start in free-fighting stance, and the attacker announces 'Mae-geri!'

2

The attacker executes a front kick, mae-geri, with the rear leg. The defender slides to the side and blocks with downward block, gedan barai.

3

The defender punches with the reverse hand, gyaku-zuki.

SIDE THRUSTING KICK
Yoko Kekomi

1

Both opponents start in free-fighting stance, and the attacker announces 'Yoko kekomi!'

2

The attacker executes a side thrusting kick, yoko kekomi, with the rear leg. The defender slides to the side and blocks with outside block, soto-uke.

3

The defender punches with the reverse hand, gyaku-zuki.

ROUNDHOUSE KICK
Mawashi-geri

1

Both opponents start in free-fighting stance, and the attacker announces 'Mawashi-geri!'

2

The attacker executes a roundhouse kick, mawashi-geri, with the rear leg. The defender slides back and blocks with inside block, uchi-uke.

3

The defender punches with the reverse hand, gyaku-zuki.

BACK KICK
Ushiro-geri

1

Both opponents start in free-fighting stance, and the attacker announces 'Ushiro-geri!'

2

The attacker executes a back kick, ushiro-geri, with the rear leg. The defender slides to the side and blocks with outside block, soto-uke.

3

The defender punches with the reverse hand, gyaku-zuki.

TRAINING TIPS

■ Try using different blocks. The ones shown are recommended, but you should feel free to find what works best for you. It is good to have a variety of defenses in your arsenal so that you do not become predictable, but remember that whatever you do has to actually work. When it comes to your grading examination, it is better to keep it simple than to try something difficult and get it wrong.

■ Beware of blocking with an open hand, particularly when defending against the kicks. You are often better off getting kicked in the body than having a foot collide with your open fingers. Keeping a closed fist will protect your hands.

■ Kicks are powerful, so try to step out of the way rather than using brute force to block them. Front kick is particularly dangerous, and trying to directly parry it with your forearm could even result in a broken arm.

■ Be mindful of distancing and targeting. If you find that your attacks are falling short, you should increase your range. When kicking, this is done by pushing the hips further forward toward the target. When punching, this can be done by sliding your front foot nearer to the target or by using a longer and deeper stance.

■ Control your anger. To attack and defend effectively you need to be strong and confident while keeping a focused mind. If you get angry, you will lose that focus.

APPENDICES

Grading Syllabus

WHITE BELT GRADING SYLLABUS	
Basics	
Stepping punch	Oi-zuki
Rising block	Age-uke
Outside block	Soto-uke
Inside block	Uchi-uke
Front kick	Mae-geri
Kata	
Kihon Kata (Taikyoku Shodan)	
Kumite	
Five-step sparring	Gohon kumite

ORANGE BELT GRADING SYLLABUS

Basics

Stepping punch	Oi-zuki
Rising block	Age-uke
Outside block	Soto-uke
Inside block	Uchi-uke
Knife-hand block	Shuto-uke
Front kick	Mae-geri
Side thrusting kick	Yoko kekomi
Side rising kick	Yoko keage

Kata

Kihon Kata (Taikyoku Shodan)

Heian Shodan

Kumite

Five-step sparring	Gohon kumite

RED BELT GRADING SYLLABUS

Basics

Triple punch	Sanbon tsuki
Rising block, reverse punch	Age-uke, gyaku-zuki
Outside block, reverse punch	Soto-uke, gyaku-zuki
Inside block, reverse punch	Uchi-uke, gyaku-zuki
Knife-hand block	Shuto-uke
Front kick	Mae-geri
Side thrusting kick	Yoko kekomi
Side rising kick	Yoko keage

Kata

Kihon Kata (Taikyoku Shodan)

Heian Shodan

Heian Nidan

Kumite

Five-step sparring	Gohon kumite

YELLOW BELT GRADING SYLLABUS

Basics

Triple punch	Sanbon tsuki
Rising block, reverse punch, downward block	Age-uke, gyaku-zuki, gedan barai
Outside block, elbow strike	Soto-uke, empi-uchi
Inside block, reverse punch	Uchi-uke, gyaku-zuki
Knife-hand block, spear-hand strike	Shuto-uke, nukite
Consecutive front kicks	Mae ren-geri
Side thrusting kick	Yoko kekomi
Side rising kick	Yoko keage

Kata

Kihon Kata (Taikyoku Shodan)

Heian Shodan

Heian Nidan

Heian Sandan

Kumite

One-step sparring	Ippon kumite
Head-level stepping punch	Jodan oi-zuki
Stomach-level stepping punch	Chudan oi-zuki

GREEN BELT GRADING SYLLABUS

Basics

Triple punch	Sanbon tsuki
Rising block, reverse punch, downward block	Age-uke, gyaku-zuki, gedan barai
Outside block, elbow strike, back-fist strike	Soto-uke, empi-uchi, uraken-uchi
Inside block, jabbing punch, reverse punch	Uchi-uke, kizami-zuki, gyaku-zuki
Knife-hand block, jabbing front kick, spear-hand strike	Shuto-uke, kizami mae-geri, nukite
Consecutive front kicks	Mae ren-geri
Side thrusting kick	Yoko kekomi
Side rising kick	Yoko keage
Roundhouse kick	Mawashi-geri

Kata

Kihon Kata (Taikyoku Shodan)

Heian Shodan

Heian Nidan

Heian Sandan

Heian Yondan

Kumite

One-step sparring	Ippon kumite
Head-level stepping punch	Jodan oi-zuki
Stomach-level stepping punch	Chudan oi-zuki
Front kick	Mae-geri
Side thrusting kick	Yoko kekomi

PURPLE BELT GRADING SYLLABUS

Basics

Triple punch	Sanbon tsuki
Rising block, reverse punch, downward block	Age-uke, gyaku-zuki, gedan barai
Outside block, elbow strike, back-fist strike, reverse punch	Soto-uke, empi-uchi, uraken-uchi, gyaku-zuki
Inside block, jabbing punch, reverse punch	Uchi-uke, kizami-zuki, gyaku-zuki
Knife-hand block, jabbing front kick, spear-hand strike	Shuto-uke, kizami mae-geri, nukite
Consecutive front kicks	Mae ren-geri
Side thrusting kick	Yoko kekomi
Side rising kick	Yoko keage
Roundhouse kick	Mawashi-geri

Kata

Kihon Kata (Taikyoku Shodan)

Heian Shodan

Heian Nidan

Heian Sandan

Heian Yondan

Heian Godan

Kumite

One-step sparring	Ippon kumite
Head-level stepping punch	Jodan oi-zuki
Stomach-level stepping punch	Chudan oi-zuki
Front kick	Mae-geri
Side thrusting kick	Yoko kekomi

PURPLE AND WHITE BELT GRADING SYLLABUS

Basics

Triple punch	Sanbon tsuki
Rising block, reverse punch, downward block	Age-uke, gyaku-zuki, gedan barai
Outside block, elbow strike, back-fist strike, reverse punch, downward block	Soto-uke, empi-uchi, uraken-uchi, gyaku-zuki, gedan barai
Inside block, jabbing punch, reverse punch, downward block	Uchi-uke, kizami-zuki, gyaku-zuki, gedan barai
Knife-hand block, jabbing front kick, spear-hand strike	Shuto-uke, kizami mae-geri, nukite
Consecutive front kicks	Mae ren-geri
Side thrusting kick	Yoko kekomi
Side rising kick	Yoko keage
Roundhouse kick	Mawashi-geri
Back kick	Ushiro-geri

Kata

Kihon Kata (Taikyoku Shodan)

Heian Shodan

Heian Nidan

Heian Sandan

Heian Yondan

Heian Godan

Tekki Shodan

Kumite

One-step sparring	Ippon kumite
Head-level stepping punch	Jodan Oi-zuki
Stomach-level stepping punch	Chudan Oi-zuki
Front kick	Mae-geri
Side thrusting kick	Yoko kekomi
Roundhouse kick	Mawashi-geri

BROWN BELT GRADING SYLLABUS

Basics

Triple punch	Kizami-zuki, oi-zuki, gyaku-zuki
Front kick combination	Mae-geri, oi-zuki, gyaku-zuki
Side thrusting kick combination	Yoko kekomi, uraken-uchi, gyaku-zuki
Roundhouse kick combination	Mawashi-geri, uraken-uchi, gyaku-zuki
Back kick combination	Ushiro-geri, uraken-uchi, gyaku-zuki

Kata

Kihon Kata (Taikyoku Shodan)

Heian Shodan

Heian Nidan

Heian Sandan

Heian Yondan

Heian Godan

Tekki Shodan

Bassai Dai

Kumite

One-step free sparring	Jiyu ippon kumite
Head-level stepping punch	Jodan oi-zuki
Stomach-level stepping punch	Chudan oi-zuki
Front kick	Mae-geri
Side thrusting kick	Yoko kekomi
Roundhouse kick	Mawashi-geri
Back kick	Ushiro-geri

BLACK BELT GRADING SYLLABUS

Basics

Triple punch	Kizami-zuki, oi-zuki, gyaku-zuki
Front kick combination	Mae-geri, oi-zuki, gyaku-zuki
Side thrusting kick combination	Yoko kekomi, uraken-uchi, gyaku-zuki
Roundhouse kick combination	Mawashi-geri, uraken-uchi, gyaku-zuki
Back kick combination	Ushiro-geri, uraken-uchi, gyaku-zuki
Four-kick combination	Mae-geri, yoko kekomi, mawashi-geri, ushiro-geri, uraken-uchi, gyaku-zuki
Standing kicks	Mae-geri, yoko kekomi, ushiro-geri
Black belt combination	

Kata

Kihon Kata (Taikyoku Shodan)

Heian Shodan

Heian Nidan

Heian Sandan

Heian Yondan

Heian Godan

Tekki Shodan

Choose one from

Bassai Dai, Kanku Dai, Jion, Empi, Hangetsu

Kumite

One-step free sparring	Jiyu ippon kumite
Head-level stepping punch	Jodan oi-zuki
Stomach-level stepping punch	Chudan oi-zuki
Front kick	Mae-geri
Side thrusting kick	Yoko kekomi
Roundhouse kick	Mawashi-geri
Back kick	Ushiro-geri
Free sparring	Jiyu-kumite

Shotokan Karate Kata

太極初段 KIHON KATA (TAIKYOKU SHODAN)

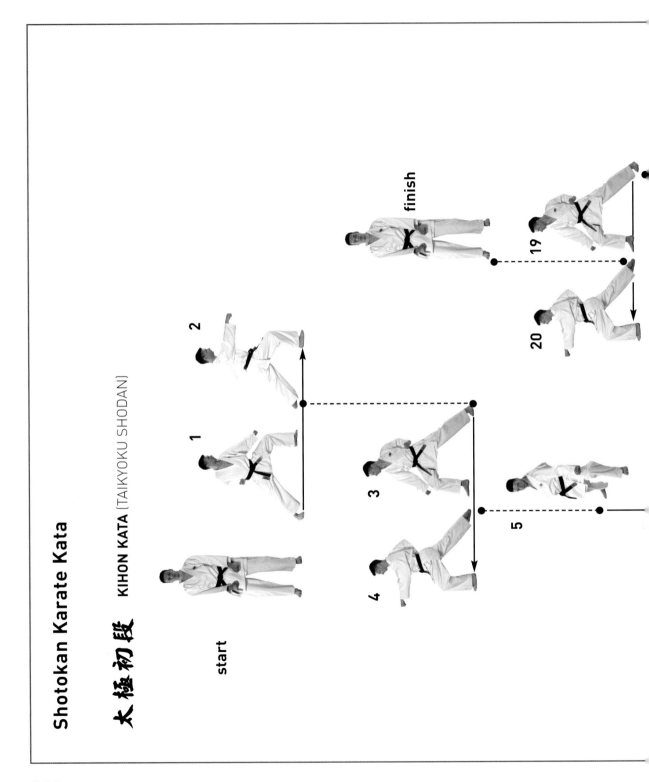

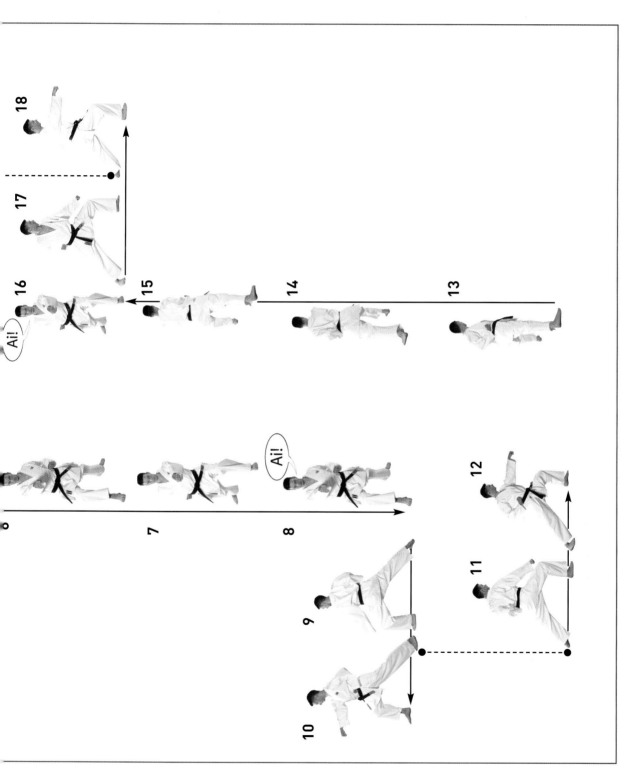

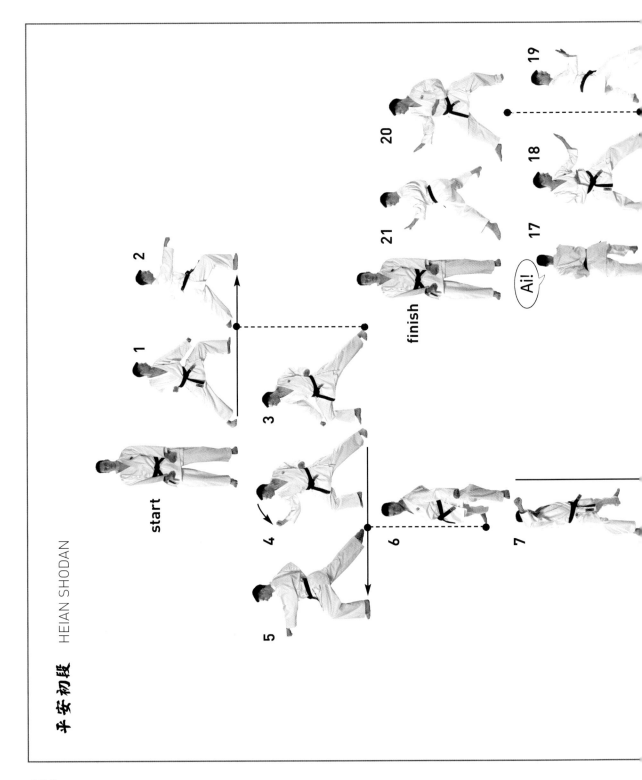

平安初段 HEIAN SHODAN

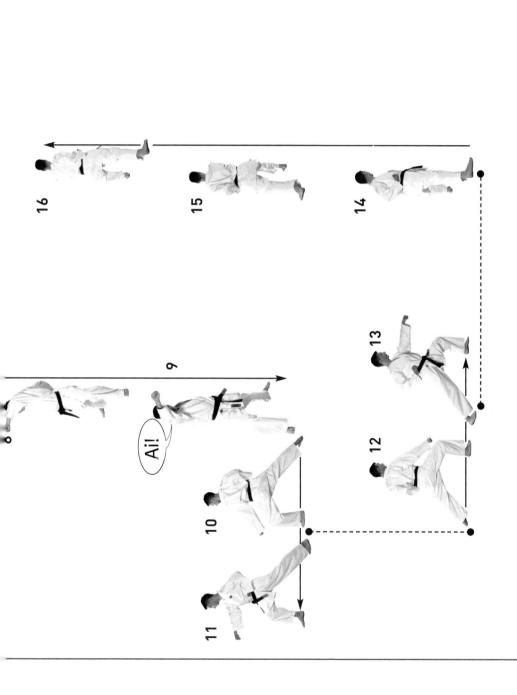

平安二段 HEIAN NIDAN

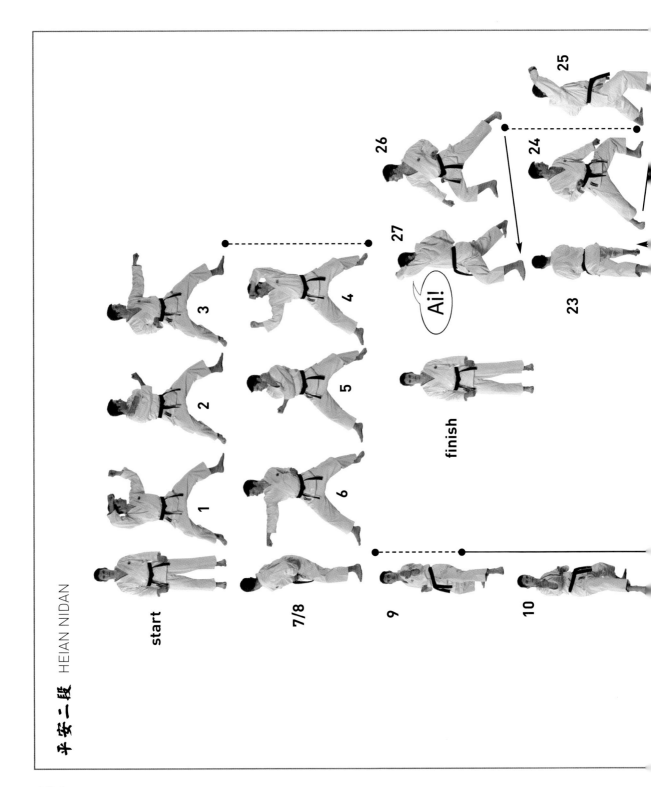

start

1

2

3

4

5

6

7/8

9

10

23

24

25

26

27

Ai!

finish

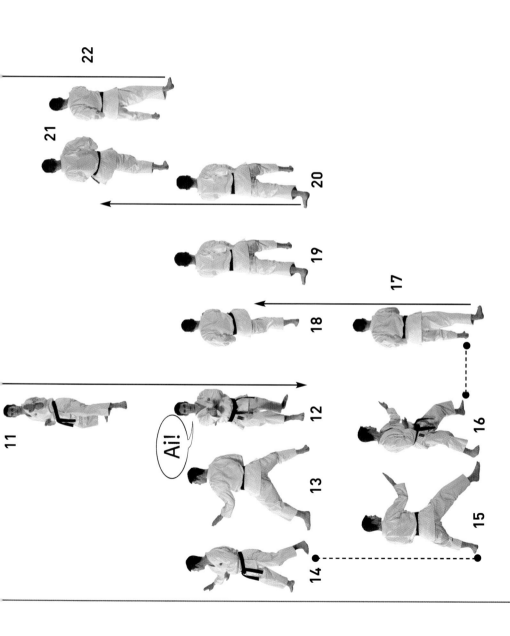

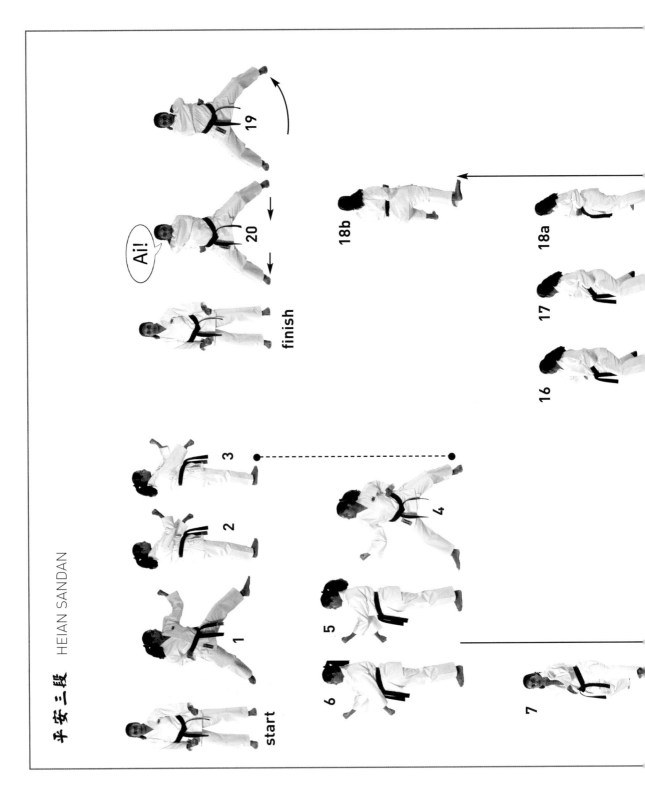

平安三段 HEIAN SANDAN

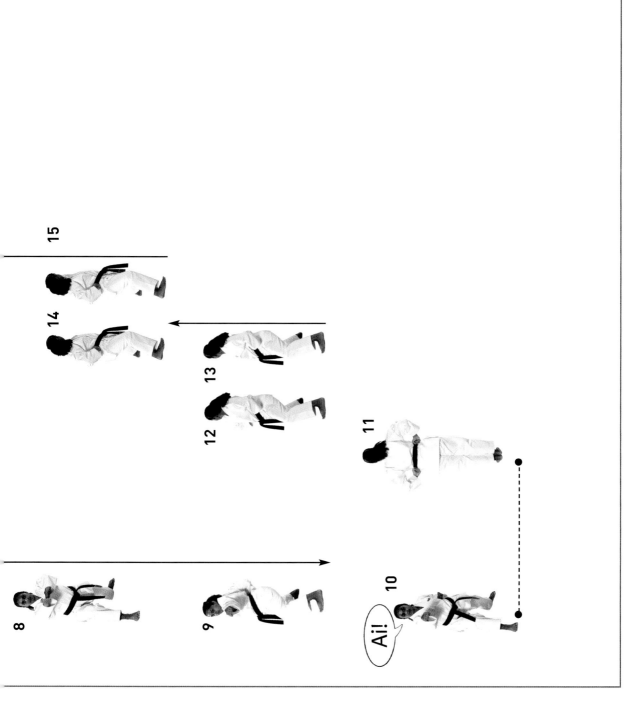

平安四段 HEIAN YONDAN

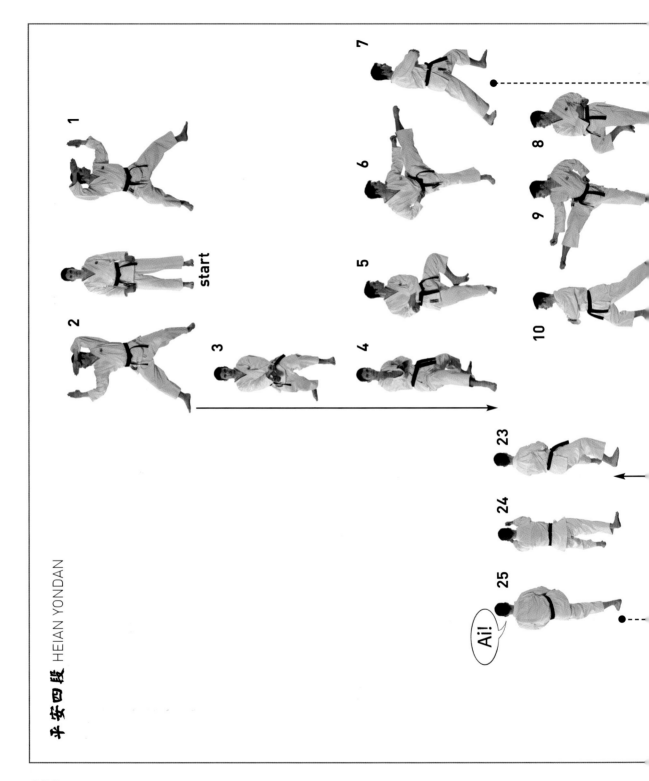

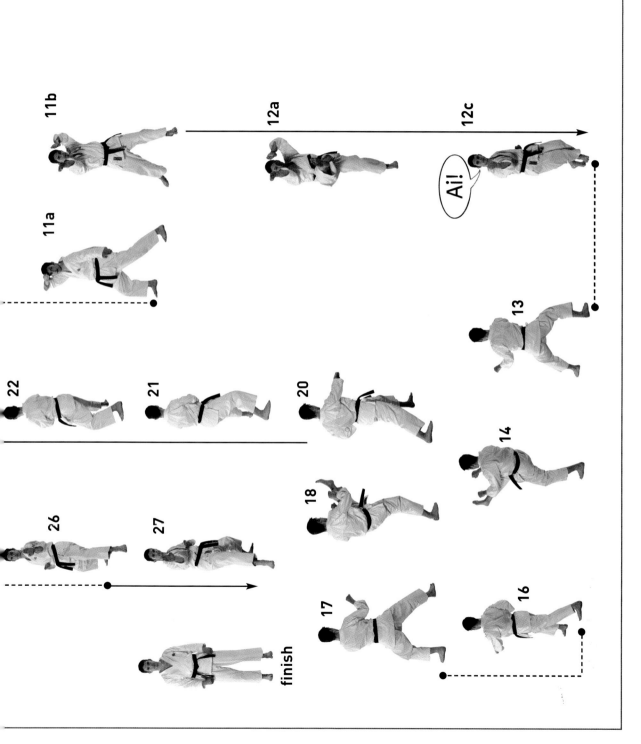

平安五段 HEIAN GODAN

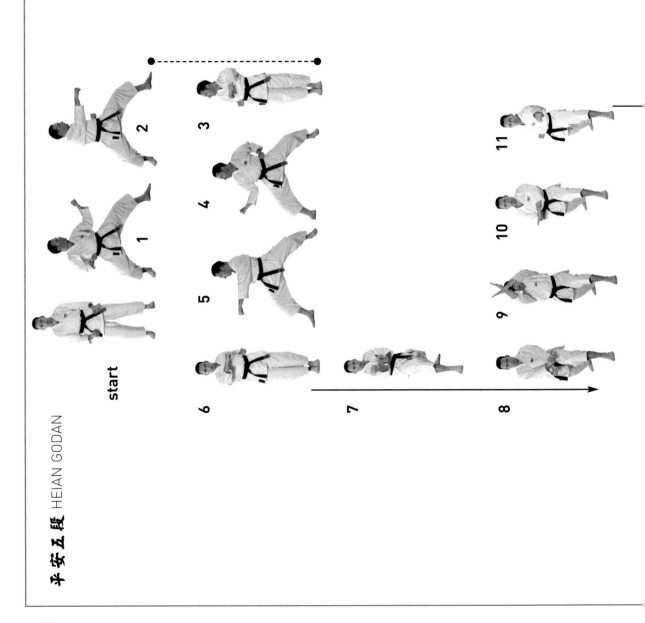

start

1

2

3

4

5

6

7

8

9

10

11

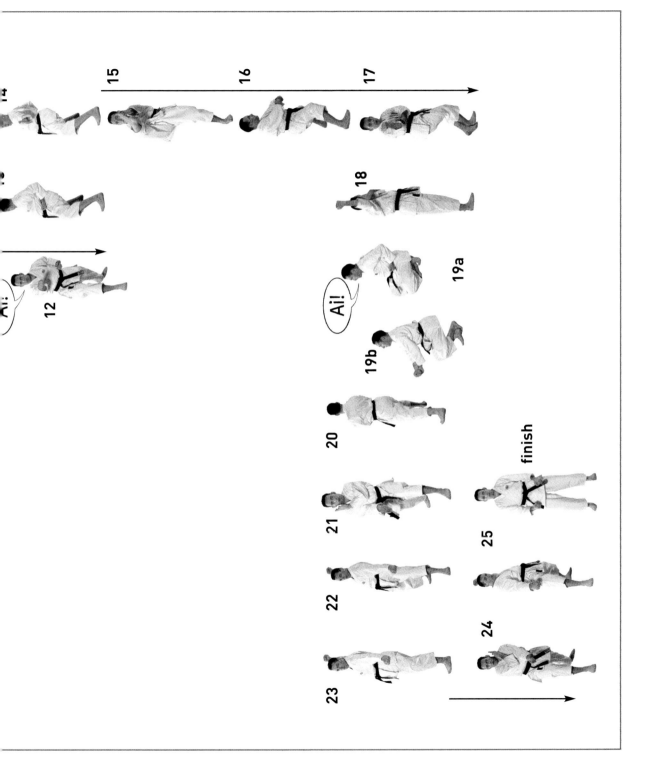

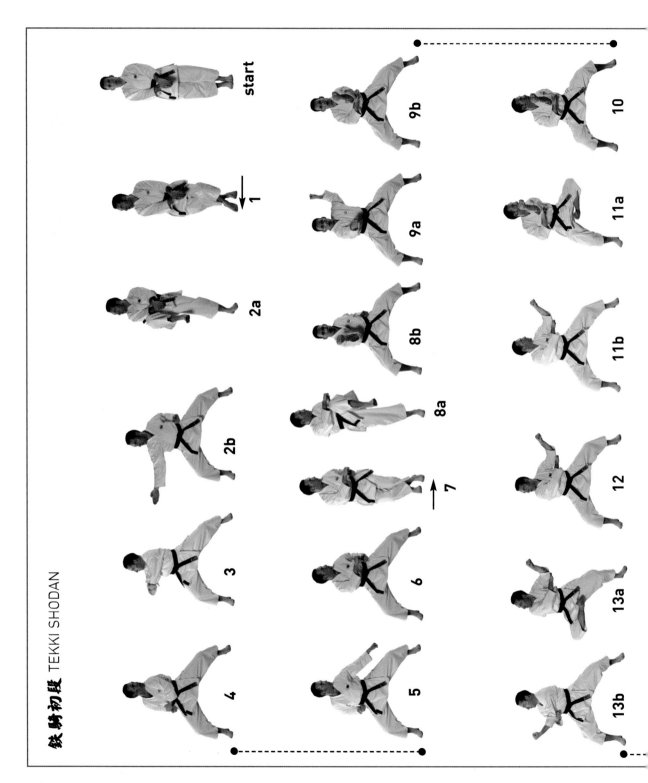

鉄騎初段 TEKKI SHODAN

start

1

2a

2b

3

4

8a

7

6

5

9b

9a

8b

10

11a

11b

12

13a

13b

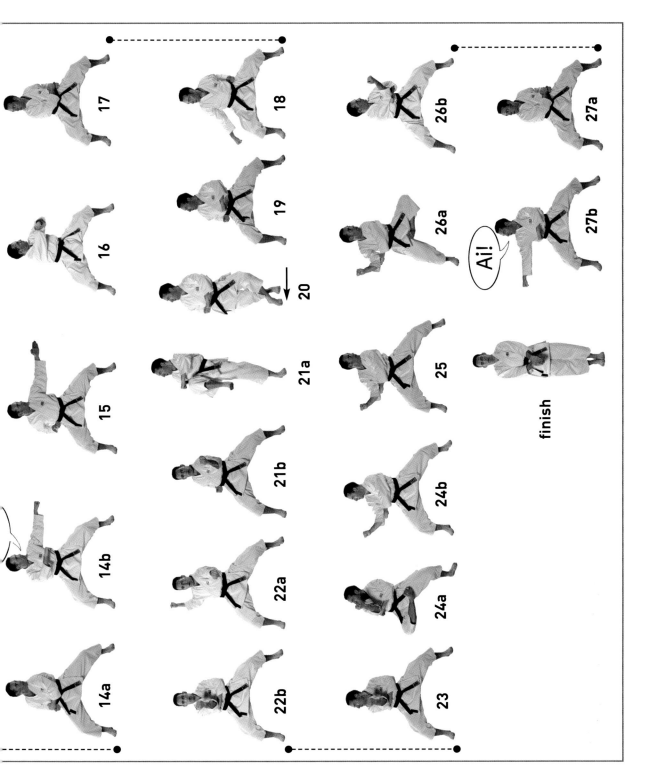

拔塞大 BASSAI DAI

start

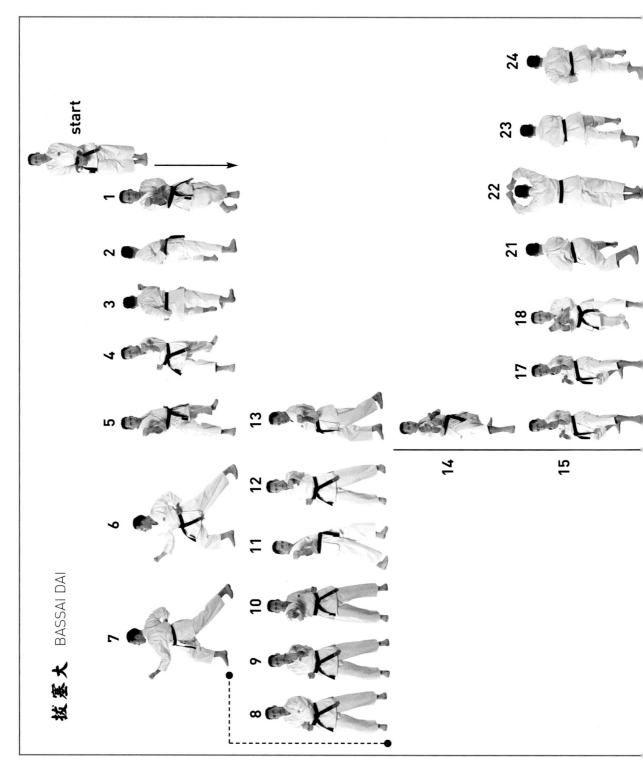

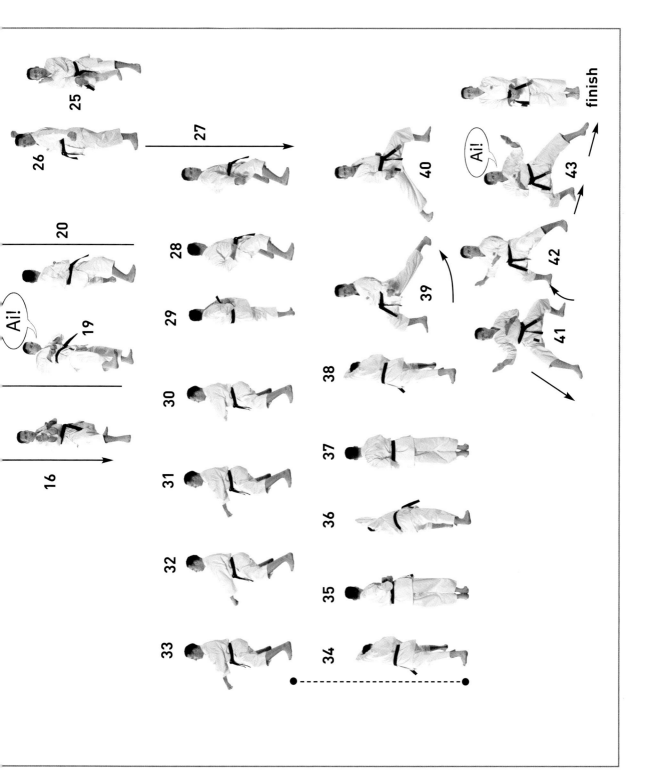

BIBLIOGRAPHY

Abernethy, I., *Bunkai Jutsu*, Neth Publishing, 2002.

Clayton, B. D., *Shotokan's Secret*, Ohara Publications Inc., 2004.

Egami, S., *The Heart of Karate-do*, Kodansha, 2000.

Funakoshi, G., *Karate Do Kyohan*, Kodansha, 1973.

Funakoshi, G., *Karate Do, My Way of Life*, Kodansha, 1975.

Funakoshi, G., *Karate Do Nyumon*, Kodansha, 1988.

Haines, B. A., *Karate's History and Traditions*, Tuttle, 1995.

Nakayama, M., *Best Karate Volume 5*, Kodansha, 1979.

Nakayama, M., *Best Karate Volume 6*, Kodansha, 1979.

Nakayama, M., *Dynamic Karate*, Kodansha, 1987.

GLOSSARY

Age-uke	Rising block
Bassai dai	Brown belt kata translated as 'escape from a castle, primary version' (literally translated as 'fortress extraction, large')
Budo	Way of the warrior
Chudan	Stomach level
Ch'uan fa	Chinese boxing (literally translated as 'fist way')
Dachi	Stance
Dogi	Karate uniform
Dojo	Karate training hall, literally translated as 'place of the way'
Dojo kun	School code, recited in many karate schools at the beginning or end of class
Empi-uchi	Elbow strike. Empi can also be written 'enpi,' but it is always pronounced empi.
Gedan barai	Downward block (literally translated as 'lower-level sweep')
Gi	Karate uniform. Short version of dogi.
Gohon kumite	Five-step sparring
Gyaku-zuki	Reverse punch
Hajime	Begin
Heian	Peace. Shotokan karate contains five Heian kata: Heian Shodan, Heian Nidan, Heian Sandan, Heian Yondan and Heian Godan.
Heiko-dachi	Parallel-feet stance
Heisoku-dachi	Formal attention stance (literally translated as 'closed feet stance')

Ippon kumite	One-step sparring
Jiyu ippon kumite	Free one-step sparring
Jiyu kumite	Free sparring
Jodan	Head level
Juji-uke	Cross block
Kagi-zuki	Hook punch
Kanji	Type of ideogram used in the Japanese writing system, literally translated as 'Han characters' in reference to the Chinese Han Dynasty
Kata	'Form' or 'pattern.' In the context of karate, this means a sequence of prearranged techniques against imaginary opponents.
Keimochi	Member of the Okinawan nobility
Keri	Kick. When it follows another word, the sound changes to geri, as in mae-geri, mawashi-geri and so on.
Kiai	A martial shout (literally translated as 'spirit unity')
Kiba-dachi	Horse-riding stance
Kihon	Basic
Kime	Literally translated as 'decision.' To focus all your energy into a technique.
Kizami-zuki	Jabbing punch
Kokutsu-dachi	Back stance
Kosa-dachi	Crossed leg stance
Kumite	Sparring
Mae-geri	Front kick
Manji-uke	Swastika block

Mawashi-geri	Roundhouse kick	**Tate shuto-uke**	Vertical knife-hand block
Mawatte	Turn	**Tekki**	Iron Horse. Shotokan karate contains three Tekki kata: Tekki Shodan, Tekki Nidan and Tekki Sandan.
Mikazuki-geri	Crescent kick		
Mokuso	Meditate		
Morote-uke	Double-handed block	**Tetsui-uchi**	Hammer-hand strike
Musubi-dachi	Informal attention stance (literally translated as 'connected stance')	**Tode**	Okinawan unarmed fighting style, literally translated as 'Chinese fist'
Nagashi-uke	Passing block	**Tsukami-uke**	Grasping block
Naha-te	Okinawan unarmed fighting style from the port town of Naha	**Tsuki**	Punch (literally translated as 'thrust'). The Tsu sound changes whenever it follows another word, so tsuki becomes zuki in oi-zuki, gyaku-zuki and so on.
Nami gaeshi-geri	Returning wave kick		
Naore	Relax (literally translated as 'put back into place')		
Nukite-uchi	Spear-hand strike	**Uchi-uke**	Inside block
Oi-zuki	Stepping punch (literally translated as a 'chasing punch')	**Ude-uke**	Forearm block
		Uke	Usually interpreted as a block in karate but literally translated it means 'reception.' Judo and ju jitsu practitioners call the person who is thrown the uke the receiver. Karate practitioners might refer to the defender as the ukete, the receiving hand.
Pinan	Original Okinawan name for Heian, meaning 'peace'		
Randori	Literally translated as 'disordered engagement'		
Rei	Bow		
Samurai	Japanese feudal lord		
Sanbon kumite	Three-step sparring	**Uraken-uchi**	Back-fist strike
Seiretsu	Line up	**Ushiro-geri**	Back kick
Sensei	Teacher	**Yama-zuki**	Mountain punch
Shiai kumite	Tournament sparring	**Yame**	Stop
Shizen-tai	Literally translated as 'natural body'	**Yasume**	Rest
		Yoi	Ready
Shodan	First level. A first-degree black belt is called a shodan.	**Yoi-dachi**	Ready stance
		Yoko keage	Side rising kick
Shuri	Historic capital of Okinawa influential in the creation of karate	**Yoko kekomi**	Side thrusting kick
		Yori ashi	Sliding foot movement where the front foot moves first
Shuri-te	Okinawan unarmed fighting style from the royal city of Shuri		
		Zenkutsu-dachi	Front stance
Shuto-uchi	Knife-hand strike		
Shuto-uke	Knife-hand block		
Soto-uke	Outside block		

INDEX